£8.99

IT

Learning to Pass

CLAiT Plus (2006)

...nd using a database

Unit 3

Ruksana Patel
& Penny Hill

www.heinemann.co.uk
✓ Free online support
✓ Useful weblinks
✓ 24 hour online ordering

01865 888058

D0332440

Heinemann Educational Publishers
Halley Court, Jordan Hill, Oxford OX2 8EJ
Part of Harcourt Education

Heinemann is the registered trademark of
Harcourt Education Limited

Text © Ruksana Patel and Penny Hill 2005

First published 2005

10 09 08 07 06 05
10 9 8 7 6 5 4 3 2 1

British Library Cataloguing in Publication Data is available
from the British Library on request.

10-digit ISBN: 0 43546344 6
13-digit ISBN: 978 0 43546344 1

Typeset by TechType, Abingdon, Oxon
Original illustrations © Harcourt Education Limited, 2005
Cover design by Wooden Ark
Printed in the UK by Bath Press
Cover photo: © Getty Images

Acknowledgements

Every effort has been made to contact copyright holders of material reproduced in this
book. Any omissions will be rectified in subsequent printings if notice is given to the
publishers.

Microsoft product screenshots reprinted with permission from Microsoft Corporation.

The authors would like to thank Abdul Patel, Stephe and Mur Cove for working through
the book and the tasks and for providing invaluable feedback. Thank you to Brian
and Rebecca Hill, Fayaz and Fozia Roked for their help, encouragement and support.
Thank you to Gavin Fidler and Lewis Birchon for their invaluable input which has
improved the quality of the book and for their constant support, advice and patience
during the production process. And finally, we would like to thank each other for "being
there for each other".

Contents

An introduction to the qualification can be found
on the CD-ROM that accompanies this book.

Who this book is suitable for:

This book is suitable for:

- anyone working towards:
    - OCR Level 2 Certificate/Diploma for IT Users (New CLAiT)
    - OCR ITQ qualification
- use as a self-study workbook, the user should work through the book from start to finish
- tutor-assisted workshops or tutor-led groups
- anyone wanting to learn to extend their skills of Microsoft Office Access 2003. Default settings are assumed. Although this book is based on Access 2003, it may also be suitable for users of Access 2002 (XP) and Access 2000. Note that a few of the skills may be slightly different and some screen prints will not be identical.

UNIT 3: Creating and using a database

How to use this book

This book is written for one unit of the syllabus. Separate books are available for each of the other units. A compendium book containing units 1, 2 and 3 is also available.

In Unit 3, you need to create a new database, enter approximately 10 records, create a report, create labels, import a generic datafile of about 100 records, update it, create queries and reports from it.

This book is divided into six sections:

- in Section 1 you will learn how to create a new database
- in Section 2 you will learn how to create tabular reports and how to create labels
- in Section 3 you will learn how to import a csv file and modify the field characteristics. You will then learn how to delete a record, replace data and amend data
- in Section 4 you will learn how to create queries using logical, range and wildcard criteria
- in Section 5 you will learn how to create a grouped report and how to format reports
- in Section 6 you will learn how to create columnar and tabular reports displaying selected fields.

You will use a software program called Microsoft Office Access 2003 which is part of Microsoft Office 2003. Access is a program that saves data as it is entered, allows different views of data and lets you search for and present data in many different ways. We will refer to it as Access from now on.

How to work through this book

This book assumes knowledge of Level 1 skills in manipulating databases using Microsoft Access 2003, and Level 1 database terms.

1 Read the explanation of a term first.

2 If there are some terms you do not understand, refer to the "Definition of terms".

3 Work through the book in sequence so that one skill is understood before moving on to the next. This ensures understanding of the topic and prevents unnecessary mistakes.

4 Read the **▶ How to...** guidelines which give step-by-step instructions for each skill. Do not attempt to work through the How to... guidelines,

but read through each point and look at the screenshots. Make sure that you understand all the instructions before moving on.

5 To make sure that you have understood how to perform a skill, work through the **Check your understanding** task following that skill. You should refer to the How to… guidelines when doing the task.

6 At the end of each section is an **Assess your skills** table. Read through these lists to find out how confident you feel about the skills that you have learned.

7 Towards the end of the book are **Quick Reference Guides**, **Build-up** and **Practice tasks**. Work through each of the tasks.

If you need help, you may refer to the How to… guidelines or **Quick Reference Guides** whilst doing the build-up tasks. Whilst working on the Practice task, you should feel confident enough to use only the **Quick Reference Guides** if you need support. These guidelines may also be used during an assessment.

8 A CD-ROM accompanies this book. On it are the files that you will need to use for the tasks. Instructions for copying the files are given on page 3. The solutions for all the tasks can be found on the CD-ROM in a folder called **L2U3SG_worked**.

Note: there are many ways of performing the skills covered in this book. This book provides guidelines that have proven to be easily understood by learners.

Preparing your work area

You are advised to prepare your user area so that you can keep your files organised.

○ Create a folder for your CLAiT Plus work.

○ In this folder, create a subfolder for all the CLAiT Plus units that you will be doing.

○ In each unit subfolder, create further subfolders. For example:

- **U3 DB working** (your working folder in which all working files will be saved)

- **L2U3DB_files** (the source files folder from the CD-ROM)

- **L2U3DB_workedcopies** (the worked copies folder also copied from the CD-ROM).

Files for this book

To work through the tasks in this book, you will need the files from the folder called **L2U3DB_files**. This folder is on the CD-ROM provided with this book. Copy this folder into your user area before you begin.

 **How to...** *copy the folder* **L2U3DB_files** *from the CD-ROM*

1 Insert the CD-ROM into the CD-ROM drive of your computer.

2 Close any windows that may be open.

3 From the desktop, double-click on the **My Computer** icon to display the **My Computer** window.

4 Double-click on the **CD drive** icon.

5 A dialogue box will open displaying the contents of the CD-ROM. Click once on the folder **L2U3DB_files**. The folder will be highlighted (usually blue).

6 In the **File and Folder Tasks** section, click on **Copy this folder**.

7 The **Copy Items** dialogue box will be displayed. In this dialogue box, click on the user area where you want to copy the folder **L2U3DB_files** to.

8 Click on the **Copy** button. The folder **L2U3DB_files** will be copied to your user area.

> **TIP!**
>
> It is advisable to copy and paste a second copy to another folder in your user area as backup.

Mouse terms

Unless otherwise instructed, always click using the left mouse button.

TERM	ACTION
Point	Move the mouse on the mousemat until the pointer appears at the required position on the screen
Click	Press and release the left mouse button once
Double-click	Quickly press the left mouse button twice, then release it
Right-click	Press and release the right mouse button once. A menu will be displayed
Hover	Position the cursor over an icon or menu item and pause. A Tool tip or a further menu item will appear
Click and drag	Used to move items. Click on an item with the left mouse button, hold the mouse button down and move the item to the required location. Release the mouse button

LEARNING OUTCOMES

In this section you will learn how to:

- create a new blank database
- create a new table in design view
- enter field names, set the data type and the field properties
- save and name a table
- enter records in datasheet view
- widen a field.

▶▶ How to... *create a new blank database*

1 Load Microsoft Access 2003.

2 Click on the **File** menu, click on **New**.

3 The task pane will be displayed on the right (Figure 3.1).

4 Click on **Blank database...**. The **File New Database** dialogue box will be displayed (Figure 3.2).

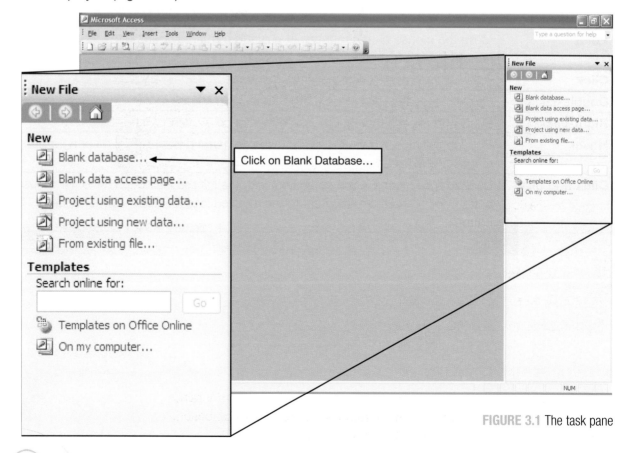

FIGURE 3.1 The task pane

5   Click on the drop-down arrow next to **Save in** and go to the databases working folder in your user area.

6   In the **File Name** box, delete **db1** and type in an appropriate filename.

7   Click on **Create**.

8   The **Database window** will be displayed (Figure 3.3). Check that **Tables** is selected in the **Objects** section on the left.

9   On the right, double-click on **Create table in Design view**.

10 The table Design view will be displayed.

11 Maximise this window.

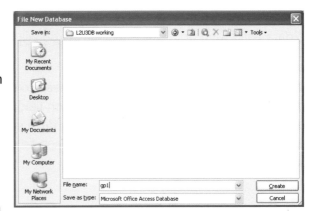

FIGURE 3.2 The File New Database dialogue box

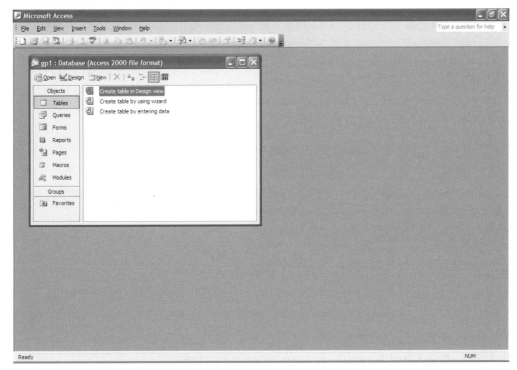

FIGURE 3.3 The Database window

Check your understanding *Create a blank database*

1   Load Access.

2   Create a blank database in your working folder called **gp1**.

3   Go to the table **Design view**.

Understanding how to create a database table

A database table is the basic component of a database, and it contains the data (records) on which all queries, reports and forms will be based. Therefore, it is very important that the table is designed correctly.

A new table is created in Design view and records are entered using either a data entry form or in Datasheet view. You will learn how to enter records in Datasheet view.

When you create a new database, you need to enter the field heading (field name) and set the data type for each field (e.g. text, number, date, currency, logic (yes/no)). A field can only have one data type. You must also set the correct field properties for each field. You will be expected to know what field properties to set.

Understanding the use and purpose of data types

Text

Text is used when you want to display text, a combination of text and numbers, and certain numbers that will not be used for calculations (e.g. telephone numbers). A text field will accept any letters and numbers. Codes are often used in databases to represent data. This helps to save space, thus improving the efficiency of the database, and it also helps to save time spent entering data. The field property can be set to accept certain codes only. This is referred to as *data validation*.

Date

A date field will only accept valid dates. Dates may be entered in any format in the table, Access will automatically convert the format to the format set in Design view when the table was designed. If you are in the UK, then, in order to provide accurate information, dates must always be set in any UK English format (day, followed by month, followed by year).

Number

Numbers might be used in a calculation. They can be displayed as whole numbers or with decimal places. Number fields will only accept numbers, letters cannot be entered into a number field.

Currency

Currency is used to display monetary amounts. The currency symbol represents the type of money used in a particular country (e.g. in the UK the currency is £ or €). Currency fields will only accept numbers. When entering data, the currency symbol need not be entered as Access will automatically display the symbol that was selected when the table was designed.

Logic

This is a Yes/No field. Access displays a logic field with a square check box – a tick represents a 'Yes' value, a blank box represents 'No'.

Understanding the Design view of a table

The first column in the top half of Design view is used to enter the field names (field headings), and the second column is used to select the appropriate data type for each field from a drop-down list. A description of the field may be entered in the third column but this is not displayed in Table, Query or Report view, therefore the description may be left blank.

The lower left half of the screen is used to set the field properties for each field. The lower right part of the screen displays more detailed information about the field properties. It is important that you take care when designing a table.

 **How to...** *enter field names, set the data type and the field properties*

1 In the table **Design view** (Figure 3.4), check that the cursor is in the first row in the **Field Name** column.

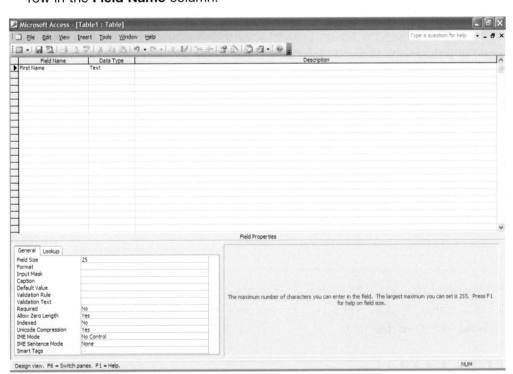

FIGURE 3.4 Design view

2 Enter the first field heading in the **Field Name** column (Figure 3.4).

3 Press the **Tab** key to move to the **Data Type** column (or click in the **Data Type** column).

4 Click on the drop-down arrow to select the data type (e.g. Text, Currency, Date/Time or Yes/No).

5 In the **Field Properties** section, set the properties as shown in the **Field Properties** table.

DATA TYPE	FIELD SIZE	FORMAT	DECIMAL PLACES
Text	Delete the default size and enter the required number based on the number of characters in the data that is to be entered in the field	–	–
Number	Click on the drop-down arrow. Select **Single** or **Double**	Click on the drop-down arrow. Select **Fixed**	Click on the drop-down arrow. Select the required number. Do not leave the setting on Auto
Date	–	Click on the drop-down arrow. Select an option (e.g. Short Date)	–

Field properties

6 Do not change any other field properties.

7 When you have entered the field name, set the data type and the field properties for the first field. Click in the second row in the **Field Name** column and repeat the process for all remaining fields (Figure 3.5).

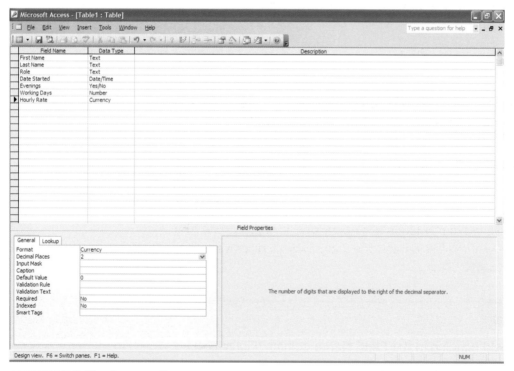

FIGURE 3.5 Setting the properties

In your database **gp1**, enter the field headings and set the data types and field properties as shown below.

FIELD HEADING	DATA TYPE	FIELD PROPERTIES
First Name	Text	25
Last Name	Text	25
Role	Text	5
Date Started	Date (Date/Time)	Short Date
Evenings	Logic field (Yes/No)	
Working Days	Number	Single, fixed, 0 decimal places
Hourly Rate	Currency	Currency, two decimal places

▶▶ How to...   *save and name the table*

1. When you have created the structure of your database table, click on the **Save** icon. The **Save As** dialogue box will be displayed (Figure 3.6).

2. Type in the required table name.

3. Click on **OK**.

4. Access will display a box asking you if you want to create a primary key. Click on **No** (primary keys are needed for databases with more than one table).

5. Click on the **View** icon  ▾ on the toolbar to switch to **Datasheet view**.

6. The field headings will be displayed as column headings, a check box will be displayed in any logic fields (a yes/no field), a zero will be displayed in any numeric fields and the £ sign will be displayed with zeros in any currency fields.

FIGURE 3.6 The Save As dialogue box

1. Save your table using the filename **surgery staff**

2. Do not create a primary key.

3. Switch to Datasheet view.

Data can be entered, edited or deleted in the table in Datasheet view or by using a *form*. Any changes made to the data using a form are automatically updated in the table. Only one record can be viewed at a time in a form.

To use a form, click on the **Forms** option in the **Objects** section in the Database window. Double-click to open the form (if a form has been created) and enter data.

You will add records directly into the table in Datasheet view. These will be automatically saved on entry.

1 Check that the cursor is flashing in the first field of row one. Enter the required data.

2 Press the **Tab** key to move to the next field and enter the required data.

3 To place a tick in a logic field box, click in the box with your mouse or press the **spacebar**.

4 In the numeric and currency fields, enter the required data. The zeros will be overtyped.

5 Press the **Tab** key to move to the next record (Figure 3.7).

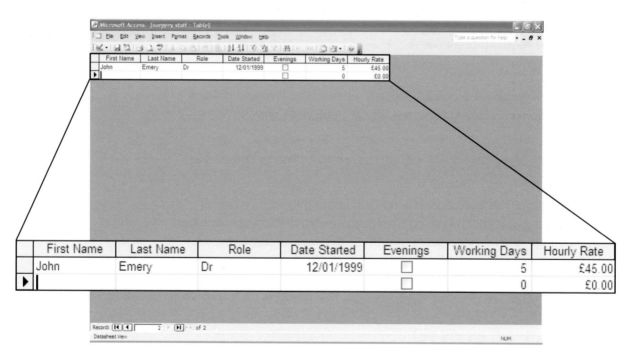

FIGURE 3.7 Record entered in Datasheet view.

 *widen a field*

TIP!

You can click and drag the width to reduce/widen columns yourself.

1 Position the cursor on the line to the right of the field heading. The cursor will turn into a double-headed arrow ⟷ . Double-click.

2 Access will adjust the column width to fit the longest line of data that is visible on the screen within the field.

Check your understanding *Enter records in Datasheet view*

1 In your database table **surgery staff**, enter the following records.

First Name	Last Name	Role	Date Started	Evenings	Working Days	Hourly Rate
John	Emery	Dr	12/01/1999	No	5	£45.00
Amy	Innes	SN	19/03/2004	Yes	3	£9.50
Robina	Darwan	OT	01/04/2001	No	2	£11.50
James	Reed	Dr	20/08/2000	Yes	1	£52.00
Elaine	Shaw	SN	12/02/2002	No	4	£14.00
Jane	Murphy	SN	06/10/2004	No	5	£10.00
Sue	Campbell	Rec	13/02/1999	Yes	5	£7.25
Idris	Adam	Phrm	20/06/2003	No	3	£19.00
Eileen	Morgan	OT	15/11/2003	No	2	£19.00
Ruth	Clarke	Rec	12/01/1999	No	5	£8.00

2 Ensure that all field headings and records are displayed in full.

3 Click on the **Spelling** icon on the toolbar to check the spelling.

4 Save your updated table keeping the name **surgery staff**.

5 For your information, the codes in the **Role** field are:

Dr   Doctor
SN   Staff Nurse
OT   Occupational Therapist
Rec   Reception Staff
Phrm Pharmacist

ASSESS YOUR SKILLS – Create a new database

By working through Section 1 you will have learnt the skills listed below. Read each item to help you decide how confident you feel about each skill:

- ○ create a new blank database
- ○ create a new table in Design view
- ○ enter field names, set the data type and the field properties
- ○ save and name a table
- ○ enter records in Datasheet view
- ○ widen a field.

If you think that you need more practice on any of the skills in the above list, go back and work through the skill(s) again.

If you feel confident, move on to Section 2.

2: Create a tabular report and create labels

LEARNING OUTCOMES

In this section you will learn how to:

- ○ create a tabular AutoReport
- ○ switch to the report Design view
- ○ sort data
- ○ delete the page number or date
- ○ insert your name and centre number
- ○ set the page orientation
- ○ insert report headers and footers
- ○ enter a report title
- ○ save a report with a specified filename
- ○ print a report
- ○ close a report
- ○ open a saved table
- ○ create labels
- ○ display headers and footers on a label report.

Simple tabular reports

A tabular report displays field names (column headings) at the top of the page with records in rows across the page. There are a number of ways to create reports. To create a tabular report in which all the records and field headings need to be displayed, the quickest method is to create an AutoReport.

If you need to create a tabular report from a small database, you are advised to follow the method below to create a tabular AutoReport. Other methods of creating reports are covered in Sections 5 and 6.

TIP!

If you have used the New Object: AutoForm icon once, the next time it may display as the last object used (e.g. **New Object: Report** ▾ or **New Object: Query** ▾).

▶▶ How to... create an AutoReport

1 With the table open in **Datasheet view**, on the toolbar, click on the drop-down arrow next to **New Object: AutoForm** ▾.

2 A drop-down list will be displayed (Figure 3.8). Click on **Report**.

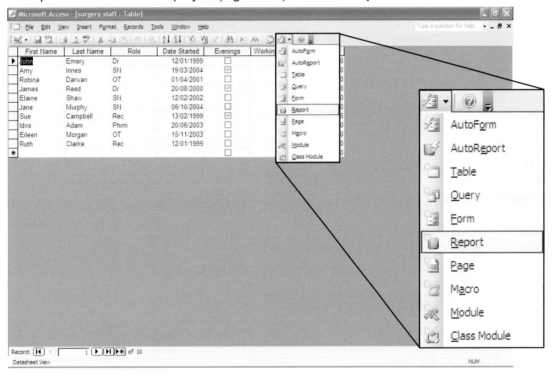

FIGURE 3.8 Selecting Report

3 The **New Report** dialogue box will be displayed (Figure 3.9).

4 Click on **AutoReport: Tabular**.

5 Click on **OK**.

6 Access will create the report automatically and will display it in Print Preview (Figure 3.10). Zoom in to the report to check that all the data is displayed in full. If any data is truncated click on the view icon 📐 ▾ to switch to the report Design view and refer to **How to... widen a field** in Section 5 on page 49.

FIGURE 3.9 The New Report dialogue box

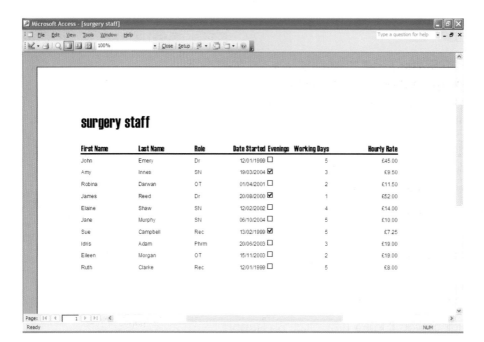

FIGURE 3.10 The report displayed in Print Preview

Check your understanding *Create a tabular AutoReport*

1   Open your database table **surgery staff**.

2   Create a tabular AutoReport to display all the fields and all records in the same order as in the table.

▶▶ How to... *switch to the report Design view*

1   In the Print Preview of the report, click on the **View** icon on the toolbar.

2   The report will be displayed in Design view (Figure 3.11).

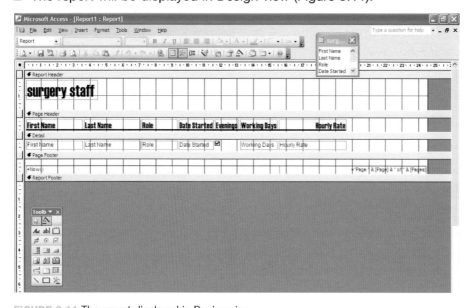

FIGURE 3.11 The report displayed in Design view

1 In Design view, click on the **Sorting and Grouping** icon . The **Sorting and Grouping** dialogue box will be displayed. The cursor will appear in the first row of the **Field/Expression** column (Figure 3.12).

2 Click on the drop-down arrow in the first row. A list of field headings will be displayed. Select the field to be sorted.

3 Click in the first row of the **Sort Order** column, click on the drop-down arrow. Select **Ascending** or **Descending** (Figure 3.13).

4 Click on the cross to close the Sorting and Grouping dialogue box.

5 Click the **Print Preview** icon to check that data has been sorted.

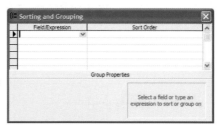

FIGURE 3.12 The Sorting and Grouping dialogue box

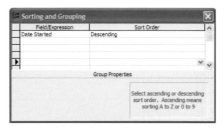

FIGURE 3.13 Sorting the field

Check your understanding *Sort data in a report*

In your **Report1** titled **Surgery Staff**, sort the data in ascending order of **Last Name**.

Headers and footers in reports

Access automatically displays the date and the number of pages in a report. Therefore you will not have to insert these but, when you preview the report, you should check that these are displayed. In Design view, the date displays as =*Now()* in a control box and the page numbers display as =''Page'' & [Page] & ''of'' & [Pages] in a control box.

> **TIP!**
>
> A *control* is a label box or a text box in a report. If you are unsure which control (box) is a label or a text box, click on the box and then press the F1 key. A tool tip will be displayed with an explanation of the type of box (control).

How to... delete the page number or date

1 In Design view, click once in the control box to be deleted. Square handles will be displayed around the control box.

2 Press the **Delete** key.

How to... insert your name and centre number

You can use label boxes in Design view to enter your name and centre number. To enter text labels, the Page Header/Page Footer and the Toolbox need to be displayed (Figure 3.14).

1 If the Page Header/Page Footer are not displayed, click on the **View** menu, click on **Page Header/Footer**.

2 If the Toolbox is not displayed, click on the **View** menu, click on **Toolbox** (Figure 3.14).

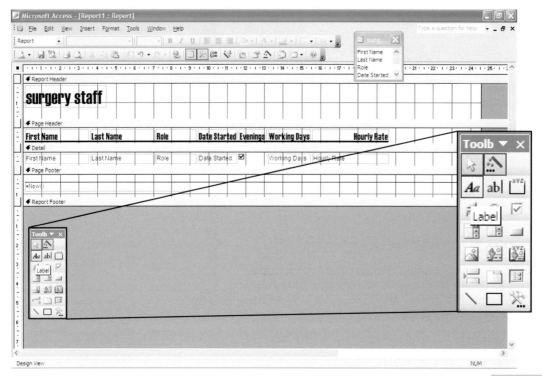

FIGURE 3.14 The Toolbox

3 From the Toolbox, select the **Label** icon Aa.

4 Draw a text box in the Page Footer area.

5 Type in the required information (Figure 3.15).

TIP!

Do not select the text box icon which displays ab.

TIP!

To format the font type and size of this label refer to How to… change the font size and How to… change the font type in section 5 on pages 50 and 51.

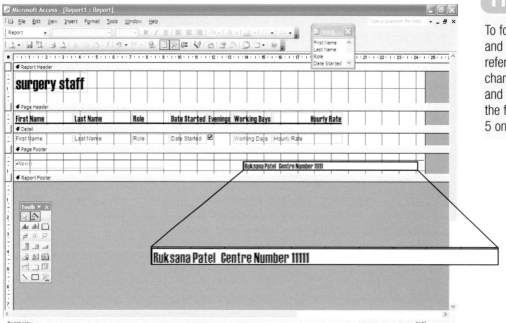

FIGURE 3.15 Drawing a text box and entering data

1   In the footer of your **Report1**, titled **surgery staff**, check that the date field is displayed.

2   Delete the page number.

3   Create a label box and enter your name and centre number in the footer.

▶▶ *How to...* set the page orientation

1   Click on the **File** menu, click on **Page Setup**.

2   The **Page Setup** dialogue box will be displayed.

3   Click on the **Page** tab and select **Portrait** or **Landscape**.

4   Margins can also be changed in the Page Setup dialogue box. Click on the **Margins** tab. Change the top, bottom, left and right margins as required.

5   Click on **OK**.

Set the orientation of your **Report1** titled **surgery staff** to **landscape**.

▶▶ *How to...* widen the report title control box and enter a report title

1   In the report Design view, click on the report title. Square handles will be displayed around the control box.

2   Click and drag the square handle on the right of the control box further to the right to widen the control box.

3   Click in the box for the report title. A cursor will be displayed.

4   Delete the existing title and enter the new title (Figure 3.16).

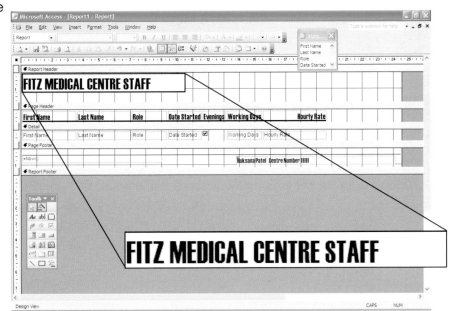

FIGURE 3.16 Entering the new title

FIGURE 3.17 The Save As dialogue box

▶▶ How to... save a report with a specified name

1 Click on the **File** menu, click on **Save**.

2 The **Save As** dialogue box will be displayed (Figure 3.17).

3 Delete the existing name and enter the required report name.

4 Click on **OK**.

▶▶ How to... print a report

1 Before you print, always use Print Preview. Zoom in to various parts of your report to check that all the data is fully displayed.

2 Click on the **Print** icon on the toolbar (from Print Preview or Design view).

3 Always check your printout to make sure that all the data is fully displayed even if you have used Print Preview.

▶▶ How to... close a report

1 Click on the **File** menu, click on **Close**.

Check your understanding *Save and print a report*

1 In your **Report1** titled **surgery staff**, delete this title.

2 Widen the report title control box and enter the title **FITZ MEDICAL CENTRE STAFF**

3 Save your report using the filename **FITZ MEDICAL CENTRE STAFF**

4 Use Print Preview to make sure the title, field headings and all the records are fully displayed.

5 Print your report entitled **FITZ MEDICAL CENTRE STAFF**.

6 Close the report.

▶▶ How to... open a saved table

1 In the **Database window**, in the **Objects** section, click on **Tables**. The tables in your database will be displayed.

2 Double-click on the table name to open it (Figure 3.18).

TIP!

Instead of double-clicking you can click once to select the table (do not click if the table name is already highlighted), then click on **Open** 🗐 Open .

FIGURE 3.18 Opening a saved table

How to... *create labels*

1   With the table (or query) open in **Datasheet** view, on the toolbar, click on the drop-down arrow next to **New Object** .

2   A drop-down list will be displayed. Click on **Report**. The **New Report** dialogue box will be displayed (Figure 3.19).

TIP!

If you have used this icon already, it may display as **New Object: Report** .

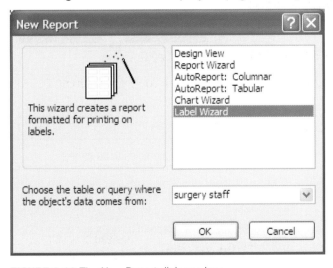

FIGURE 3.19 The New Report dialogue box

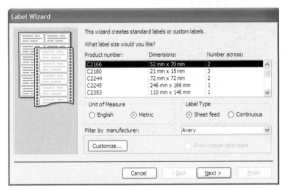

FIGURE 3.20 The Label Wizard

3   Click on **Label Wizard**. Click on **OK**.

4   The **Label Wizard** dialogue box will be displayed (Figure 3.20). If required, select the appropriate label dimensions and, if appropriate, select the correct manufacturer.

TIP!

Choose Avery 2 across, as this usually allows all the data to be fully displayed without the need to change the Page Setup.

5 Click on **Next**. In step 2, select an appropriate font name and font size (Figure 3.21). Click on **Next**.

6 In step 3, double-click in turn on each of the field headings required (Figure 3.22).

TIP!

Instead of double-clicking, you can click once on the field name, then click on the **Add** button [>].

7 To display two fields on one line, press the spacebar after you have displayed the first field. Press **Enter** to display the next field on a new line. Click on **Next**.

8 In step 4, double-click on the field(s) to be sorted (Figure 3.23).

9 Click on **Next**.

10 In step 5, enter the name of the label report (Figure 3.24). Click on **Finish**. The labels will be displayed in Print Preview.

11 To display headers and footers, click the view icon to switch to the label report Design view.

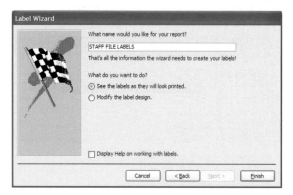

FIGURE 3.24 Entering the name of the label report

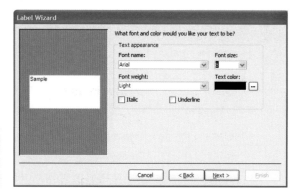

FIGURE 3.21 Selecting a font name and size

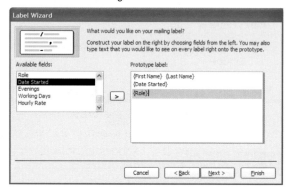

FIGURE 3.22 Selecting the field headings

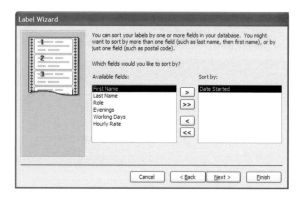

FIGURE 3.23 Selecting the fields to be sorted

TIP!

Unlike other reports, the report title does not display on a label report.

1   Using your database table **surgery staff**, create labels to be used for the staff files.

2   Display the following fields on the labels:

First Name   Last Name (separated by at least one space, on one line)
Date Started
Role

3   Sort the data in ascending order of **Date Started**.

4   Save the report using the name **STAFF FILE LABELS**

▶▶ How to... *display headers and footers on a label report*

1   In **Design view**, click on the **View** menu, click on **Page Header/Footer**, then click on the **View** menu again, click on **Page Header/Footer** (or, if the page header and page footer are already displayed, drag the grey bar to reduce/increase the page header and/or footer) (Figure 3.25).

2   If the Toolbox is not displayed click on the **View** menu, click **Toolbox**.

3   From the Toolbox, select the **Label** icon [Aa].

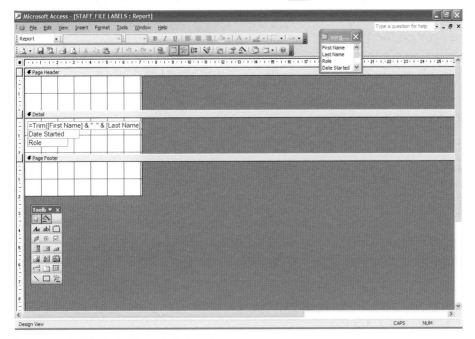

FIGURE 3.25 The Label Report Design view

4   Draw a box in the page footer area (or in the header area if required).

5   Type the required information into the text box (Figure 3.26).

TIP!

The page header/footer sections may be displayed, but there may not be sufficient room for you to create text boxes. You can resize these areas by dragging, but it is easier to alter this through the View menu.

TIP!

Reduce the depth of the page header and/or footer by clicking and dragging the bottom boundary further up.

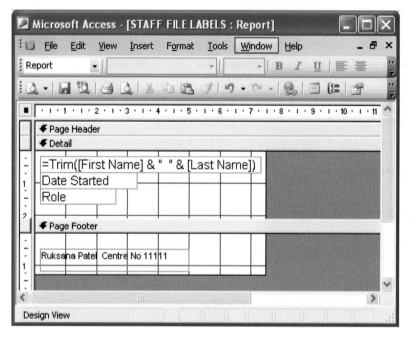

FIGURE 3.26 Footer entered and page header and footer depth reduced

6 Use Print Preview to ensure that all the labels fit on one page and that all the data is displayed in full.

7 When you click on the Print Preview icon, the message shown in Figure 3.27 may be displayed. Click on **OK** then, in Print Preview or Design view, click on the **File** menu, click on **Page Setup**, select the **Margins** tab. Reduce the left and/or right margins.

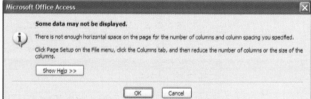

FIGURE 3.27 Some data may not be displayed

8 Optional: click on the **Columns** tab and reduce the **Column Spacing**.

9 Click on **OK**.

10 Use Print Preview again.

11 If any data is not displayed in full, click the **View** icon to go to the Design view.

12 Click on a control box in the **Detail** section, then on the **Formatting toolbar**, click on the drop-down arrow next to the **Font Size** box and select a smaller size.

13 Reduce the width of the control box and the page width.

14 Use Print Preview again.

15 Click the **Save** icon to save the updated label report.

1 In the footer of your label report titled **STAFF FILE LABELS**, create a label box and enter your name and centre number. Use Print Preview to ensure that all the data will be fully displayed on the printout.

2 Save the updated report keeping the filename **STAFF FILE LABELS**

3 Print the labels on one page. Check your printout to ensure that all the data is fully displayed.

4 Close the label report and the database table **surgery staff**.

5 Close the database **gp1**.

ASSESS YOUR SKILLS – Create a tabular report and create labels

By working through Section 2 you will have learnt the skills listed below. Read each item to help you decide how confident you feel about each skill:

- ○ create a tabular AutoReport
- ○ switch to the report Design view
- ○ sort data
- ○ delete the page number or date
- ○ insert your name and centre number
- ○ set the page orientation
- ○ insert report headers and footers
- ○ enter a report title
- ○ save a report with a specified filename
- ○ print a report
- ○ close a report
- ○ open a saved table
- ○ create labels
- ○ display headers and footers on a label report.

If you think that you need more practice on any of the skills in the above list, go back and work through the skill(s) again.

If you feel confident, move on to Section 3.

LEARNING OUTCOMES

In this section you will learn how to:

- import a csv file (generic datafile)
- modify field characteristics
- compact the database
- create a backup copy
- add a new record
- find a record
- delete a record
- amend existing data
- replace data in a field
- delete a field.

CSV

The abbreviation *csv* stands for 'comma separated values' or 'comma separated variables'. A csv file is a generic datafile, which means it can be opened and read by most software, not just by the software it was created in.

▶▶ How to... *import a csv file*

1 Load Access and create a new blank database, using a suitable filename.

2 Click on the **File** menu, click **Get External Data**, click **Import** (Figure 3.28).

TIP!

Maximise the Database Window.

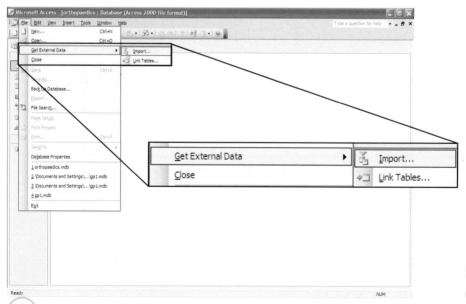

FIGURE 3.28 Importing a csv file

3 The **Import** dialogue box will be displayed.

4 Click on the drop-down arrow next to the **Look in** box. Locate the user area where the csv file is saved. There may be no files displayed at this point.

5 Click on the drop-down arrow to the right of the **Files of type** box. Scroll down the list and select **Text Files** (Figure 3.29).

6 In the main window, click on the csv file to be imported (you must ensure that the filename is highlighted) (Figure 3.30).

7 Click on **Import**. The **Import Text Wizard** will be displayed.

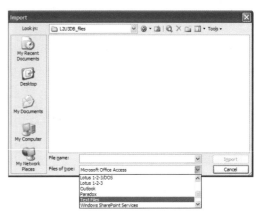

FIGURE 3.29 The Import dialogue box

FIGURE 3.30 The highlighted csv file

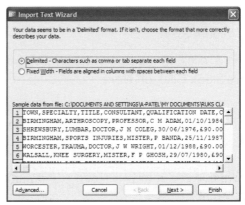

FIGURE 3.31 Step 1 of the Import Text Wizard

8 In step 1 of the Import Text Wizard, ensure **Delimited** is selected (Figure 3.31). Click on **Next**.

9 In step 2, ensure the **Comma** option is selected. Click on the drop-down arrow to the right of the **Text Qualifier** box. Select "(double speech marks). Click in the check box for **First Row Contains Field Names** (Figure 3.32).

10 Click on **Next**.

11 In step 3, check that the option for **In a New Table** is selected (Figure 3.33). Click on **Next**.

TIP!

You must select the text qualifier *before* you click in the check box.

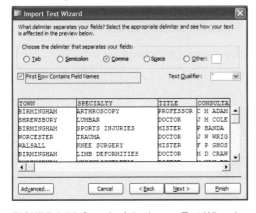

FIGURE 3.32 Step 2 of the Import Text Wizard

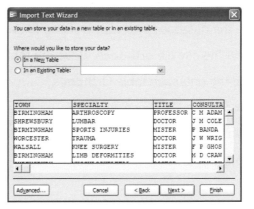

FIGURE 3.33 Step 3 of the Import Text Wizard

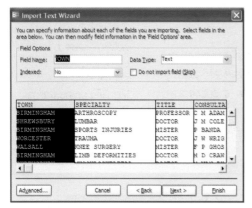

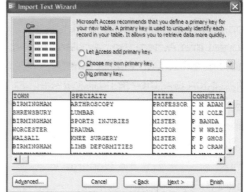

FIGURE 3.34 Step 4 of the Import Text Wizard

FIGURE 3.35 Step 5 of the Import Text Wizard

12 In step 4, click on **Next** (do not make any changes here) (Figure 3.34).

13 In step 5, click on the button for **No Primary Key** (Figure 3.35). Click on **Next**.

14 In step 6, click on **Finish** (the name of the csv file will be displayed in the **Import to Table** box) (Figure 3.36).

15 In step 7, the message **Finished importing file...** should be displayed. Click on **OK** (Figure 3.37).

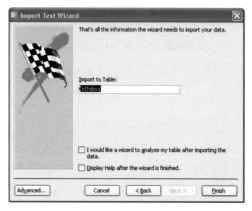

FIGURE 3.36 Step 6 of the Import Text Wizard

TIP!

If the window displays a message that there are import errors, click on **OK**, then select the table in the Database window. Click on the **Delete** key. Select the **Import Errors** table and click on the **Delete** key. Start the import process from the beginning following each step carefully.

FIGURE 3.37 Step 7 of the Import Text Wizard

Check your understanding *Import a csv file*

To do this task you will need the csv file **orthdocs**.

1 Load Access and create a new blank database.

2 Save the database into your working folder using the filename **orthopaedics**

3 Import the csv file **orthdocs**. Save the table keeping the name **Orthdocs**

4 Open the database table **Orthdocs**.

5 Maximise the Database window.

6 Widen all the fields to ensure that all the data is fully displayed.

7 Save the updated database table.

▶▶ How to... modify field characteristics

When a table is imported into Access, the Access default field properties are set. A text field size is set to 255 characters. To improve the efficiency of the database and to decrease the file size, you should view the data in the imported table, and then switch to the table Design view to modify the default characteristics. Ensure that you do not set incorrect field properties as this may cause errors in the table – you must maintain the integrity of the data.

> **TIP!**
>
> Refer to How to... enter field names, set the data type and the field properties in Section 1 if you need to (page 7).

1 Go to the Design view of the database table. Click in the **Data Type** column of the field to be modified. In the **Field Properties** section, amend the properties as required.

2 Click in the **Data Type** column of the next field to be modified. In the **Field Properties** section, amend the properties as required.

3 Repeat this process for all the other fields.

4 Click the **Save** icon.

5 Click the **View** icon to return to table Datasheet view.

Check your understanding *Modify field characteristics*

1 Modify the field properties in your database table **Orthdocs** as follows.

FIELD NAME	DATA TYPE	FIELD SIZE
TOWN	Text	25
SPECIALTY	Text	20
TITLE	Text	10
CONSULTANT	Text	25
QUALIFICATION DATE	Date	Short Date format (e.g. 30/11/1987)
CONSULTATION FEE	Currency	Currency with currency symbol, zero decimal places
WAITING DAYS	Number	Number, double, fixed format, zero decimal places

2 Save the amended database table.

▶▶ How to... compact the database (optional)

1 In the Database window, click on the **Tools** menu, click **Database Utilities**, click **Compact and Repair Database**.

2 A security warning message may be displayed (Figure 3.38). Click on **Open**.

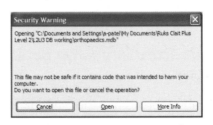

FIGURE 3.38 Security warning message

> **TIP!**
>
> Before you proceed, create a backup copy of your imported, modified database.

Check your understanding *Compact the database*

1 Compact and repair the database after you have amended the field properties.

2 Open the database table.

▶▶ *How to...* *create a backup copy of a database (optional)*

1 Click on the **File** menu, click **Back Up Database**.

2 The **Save Backup As** dialogue box will be displayed. Access will save in the same folder as the database you are working on and will suggest the original name followed by the date in American format (year, month, date).

3 In the **Save Backup As** dialogue box, click on **Save**.

4 A warning message may be displayed again. Click on **Open**.

5 The original database will reopen in the Database window.

6 In the **Objects** section, check that **Tables** is selected and that the table name is highlighted. Click on **Open**.

▶▶ *How to...* *add a new record*

New records can be added easily to a database table. However, these can only be added at the end of the table, below the last record.

1 Click on the **New Record** button in the **Record Navigation** buttons at the bottom left of the screen or click in the first column of the last row (the blank row).

2 Enter the required data in the first field. Press the **Tab** key to move to the next field.

3 Enter the required data.

4 Access automatically saves new or amended data. Only changes to the layout of a database table need to be saved.

TIP!

Although you can only add records at the end of a database table, you may find that when you close a table and open it again, the order of records may have changed (e.g. new records may no longer be displayed at the bottom). Access does this automatically. This is acceptable.

▶▶ *How to...* *find a record in a large database and delete it*

In a large database, it is advisable to use the Find facility to find a record to be deleted instead of trying to scroll through the table to locate a record.

1 Click anywhere in the field in which you want to find the data.

2 Click on the **Edit** menu, click **Find**. The **Find and Replace** dialogue box will be displayed (Figure 3.39).

3 In the **Find What** box, enter the data to be found.

4 Click on the drop-down arrow next to **Match**. A drop-down list will be displayed. Select the option for **Any Part of Field**.

5 Click on the **Find Next** button.

6 Close the **Find and Replace** dialogue box. Ensure that the cursor is displayed in the record to be deleted.

7 Click on the **Edit** menu, click **Delete Record**.

8 Access will display a message prompting you to confirm the delete.

9 Click on **Yes**.

FIGURE 3.39 The Find and Replace dialogue box

TIP!

In Access you cannot undo an action, so always check to make sure you have found the correct record – there may be several records containing similar data.

Check your understanding *Delete a record*

1 Open the imported database table **Orthdocs** if it is not already open.

2 Maximise the Table Window.

3 Widen all the fields to ensure that all the data is fully displayed.

4 Delete the record for the CONSULTANT **F S WILCOCK**

▶▶ How to... *amend existing data*

1 Ensure that all the data and the field headings are fully displayed by double-clicking between each of the field headings.

2 Click in the field to be amended. Delete the existing contents. Enter the new data.

3 Access saves an amendment automatically when you move out of the field.

4 When you have made all amendments, click in a blank row to avoid any accidental changes to data.

5 Click on the **Save** icon to save any changes to the layout of the table.

▶▶ How to... *replace data in a field*

1 Click anywhere in the field in which the data needs to be replaced.

2 Click on the **Edit** menu, click **Replace**. The **Find and Replace** dialogue box will be displayed (Figure 3.40).

3 In the **Find What** box, enter the data to be replaced. In the **Replace With** box, enter the new data.

FIGURE 3.40 The Find and Replace dialogue box

4 Check that the **Match** box displays **Whole Field** or **Any Part of Field** as appropriate for the data in the field. (If not, press the drop-down arrow and select the option required).

5 Click to place a tick in the box for **Match Case**.

6 Click on the **Replace All** button.

7 Access displays a message prompting you to confirm the replace. Click on **Yes**.

TIP!

Do not click on the **Replace** button. This will replace only one instance of the data.

Check your understanding *Replace data*

1 In your database table **Orthdocs**, amend the SPECIALTY for DR T G WOODS to **GENERAL ORTHOPAEDICS** and the WAITING DAYS to **5**

2 In the **TITLE** field, replace **all** the entries as follows:

Replace PROFESSOR with **PROF**
Replace MISTER with **MR**
Replace DOCTOR with **DR**

▶▶ How to... *delete a field*

1 Switch to the table Design view.

2 Click in the row in the field to be deleted (click in the **Field Name** or **Data Type** column).

3 Click on the **Edit** menu, click **Delete Rows**.

4 Access displays a message prompting you to confirm the delete. Click on **Yes**.

ASSESS YOUR SKILLS – Import a datafile and update a database

By working through Section 3 you will have learnt the skills listed below. Read each item to help you decide how confident you feel about each skill:

- import a csv file (generic datafile)
- modify field characteristics
- compact the database
- create a backup copy
- add a new record
- find a record
- delete a record
- amend existing data
- replace data in a field
- delete a field.

If you think that you need more practice on any of the skills in the above list, go back and work through the skill(s) again.

If you feel confident, move on to Section 4.

Understanding queries

A query is used in a database to ask questions about the data in the database table in order to find specific information. To find the specific information, appropriate *selection conditions* are entered into a query design. The term used to describe the selection conditions is *criteria*. A single criteria is referred to as a criterion.

The advantage of a query over other methods of finding specific information (e.g. filters) is that, when a database table is amended or updated, a saved query is also automatically updated. This is referred to as *live data handling*. Once a query is created and saved it can be used again, updated and resaved. Any amendments to the data in a query will automatically update the database table. Queries are often used to create reports that present information in a professional manner.

There are many ways of creating queries. Two frequently used ways are as follows:

- Creating a query using the wizard.
- Creating a query in Design view. You will learn how to create queries in Design view.

There are a number of ways to go to Design view. One frequently used method is as follows.

1 Close the database table.

2 From the Database window, click on **Queries** in the **Objects** section.

3 Click on **Create query in Design view**.

4 Click on **Open**. The **Show Table** dialogue box will be displayed.

5 Click to select the table name.

6 Click on **Add**.

7 Click on **Close**.

However, using the icons on the toolbars allows you to perform actions much more quickly (e.g. Save, Print). Similarly, it is quicker to use the **View** button on the toolbar to go to Design view. You will learn how to the use the quicker way.

Understanding query expression criteria

Range criteria

Range criteria are used to find records that are between a certain value. The range could be dates, numbers or text:

BETWEEN 30/11/85 and 20/03/87	finds all records between and including these dates.
Tip	Access will insert a # (hash) before and after each date: **#30/11/85# and #20/03/87#**
BETWEEN 30 and 45	finds all records between and including these numbers.

Logical operators

AND	Use AND to combine search criteria within one field: LONDON AND BIRMINGHAM.
	AND is also used between two values in the BETWEEN criteria: BETWEEN 30/11/85 AND 20/03/87.
OR	Use OR to find records that match any of the criteria specified: HEATHROW OR STANSTEAD OR LUTON.

Wildcard criteria

Wildcard criteria are used to find records that do not have an exact match in a field. Wildcards are used to 'pattern search':

*	Matches any number of characters. It can be used as the first or last character in the character string: ***grey***. This would find any shade of grey (e.g. silver grey, grey blue, metallic grey).
?	Matches any single alphabetic character: **b?ll**. This would find 'ball', 'bell', 'bill'.
#	Matches any single numeric character: **2#1**. This would find 201, 211, 221, 231, etc.

TIP!

Any of these operators can be combined in a query.

When you move out of a field, Access will automatically enter the word *Like* in the Criteria row and will insert speech marks before and after the criteria.

Understanding comparison operators

Where numbers or dates are used in tables, comparison operators in a query allow you to search for specific numbers or dates.

COMPARISON OPERATORS IN NUMERIC FIELDS	
>	Greater than
>=	Greater than or equal to
<	Less than
<=	Less than or equal to
<>	Not equal to or exclude

For example, <> "SALOON" and <> "ESTATE" finds all cars except SALOON and ESTATE models. <> cannot be used in wildcard searches. *Not like* should be used to exclude data if wildcard criteria are used.

COMPARISON OPERATORS IN DATE FIELDS	
>	After
>=	On or after
<	Before
<=	On or before
<>	Not equal to or exclude

TIP!

If you click in another field after entering the date criteria, you will see that Access displays a **#** (hash) sign before and after the date.

For example, **<> 01/01/2006** finds all dates except 01/01/2006. <> cannot be used in wildcard searches. *Not like* should be used to exclude data if wildcard criteria are used.

▶▶ How to... *create a new query*

1 In **Datasheet view** (with the table open), click on the drop-down arrow next to the **New Object** icon 📇 ▾.

2 A drop-down list will be displayed. From the list, click on **Query**.

3   The **New Query** dialogue box will be displayed. Check that **Design view** is highlighted.

4   Click on **OK**.

TIP!

If you have used this icon already to create a query, Access changes the icon and the tool tip to New Object: Query or New Object: Report .

Query Design view

Figure 3.41 shows the Query Design view.

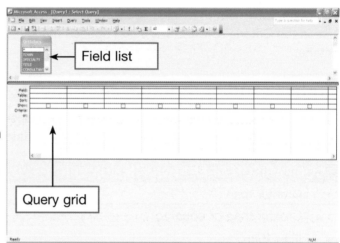

FIGURE 3.41 Query Design view

Field List box

The Field List box displays the table name in the title bar (the shaded area, usually blue) and the list of field headings in the database table.

Query grid

The Query grid consists of six rows:

○ The *Field* row displays the field name (field heading).

○ The *Table* row displays the name of the database table.

○ When clicked in, the *Sort* row displays a drop-down arrow with three sort options.

○ If the *Show* row is ticked, the field (column) will be displayed in the query result.

○ The selection condition should be entered into the *Criteria* row

○ More selection conditions may be entered into the *OR* row. You are advised not to enter any criteria in this row as there is a greater chance of error when you create queries using multiple criteria.

▶▶ **How to...**   *select field names and drag them into the Query grid*

1   Position the cursor on the database table name (usually blue) in the Field List box. Double-click. All the field names will be highlighted.

2   Click and drag the highlighted field names to the **Field** row of the first column. All the field names will be displayed in the **Field** row, the table name will be displayed in the **Table** row in all the columns, and a tick will be displayed in the **Show** row in each box (Figure 3.42).

TIP!

This method of selecting fields ensures that no fields are left out (e.g. field names that are at the bottom of the list).

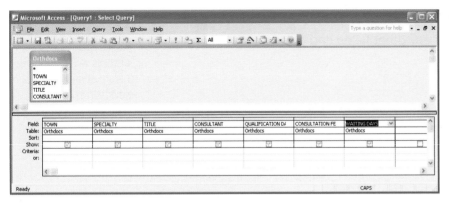

FIGURE 3.42 Field names dragged into the Query grid

▶▶ How to... *display selected fields*

Click in the **Show** box to remove the tick for the fields that you do not want to display.

▶▶ How to... *sort data in a query*

1 Click in the **Sort** row of the field to be sorted. A drop-down arrow will be displayed.

2 Click on the drop-down arrow. A list will be displayed.

3 Click on **Ascending** or **Descending**.

▶▶ How to... *enter the selection (query) criteria*

1 Click in the **Criteria** row of the field to be queried. Enter the required criteria.

2 You must enter the criteria with one hundred per cent accuracy. See the section **Understanding query expression criteria** on page 32 for information on what range, logical and wildcard criteria are and how to enter these criteria in a query. See the section **Understanding comparison operators** on page 33 for information on what comparison operators are and how to use these in queries.

▶▶ How to... *run the query*

1 Click on the **Run** icon ! on the toolbar. The results of the query will be displayed as a table in Datasheet view.

2 The number of records found in the query will be displayed in the **Record Navigation** buttons at the bottom left of the screen.

▶▶ How to... *create a query using two criteria*

1 Click in the **Criteria** row of the first field to be queried. Enter the selection criteria.

TIP!

Another way to select fields to drop into the Query grid is to double-click on each field name.

TIP!

In a query or a report, you do not need to show a field in which you entered selection criteria.

TIP!

In the Criteria row, text can be entered in upper or lower case.

TIP!

Increase the field width before you enter the query criteria so that the criteria are fully displayed. You can also increase the width after you enter the criteria.

2 Click in the **Criteria** row of the second field to be queried.

3 Click in the **Criteria** row of any other fields and enter the selection criteria.

TIP!

Notice that Access displays **#** (hash) signs before and after some selection criteria (e.g. dates) when you move out of a field.

TIP!

When creating queries with multiple criteria, enter the criteria in one field, then click on the **Run** icon ♥ to run the query. This will enable you to check that the criterion entered is correct and that the correct records are found. Click on the **View** button on the toolbar to return to Query Design view and enter the next criterion. Click on the **Run** icon again to check the accuracy of the second criterion, and so on.

▶▶ How to... *save a new query with a specified name*

1 Click on the **File** menu, click **Save**. The **Save As** dialogue box will be displayed.

2 Delete any existing text and enter the required query name.

3 Click on **OK**.

Check your understanding *Create a query using range and logical criteria*

1 In your database table **Orthdocs**, create a new query.

2 Using **range** criteria, find all the consultants whose WAITING DAYS are **between 5 and 15**

3 Using **logical** criteria, find all the consultants whose SPECIALTY is **LUMBAR or GENERAL ORTHOPAEDICS**

4 Save the query as **Lumbar + GenOrth 5-15 days**

5 Run your query.

6 Check that the records found match the criteria you entered. The query result should display 26 records. If necessary, return to Query Design view (see **How to... return to Query Design view** on page 38).

7 Your query criteria should be similar to that shown in Figure 3.43.

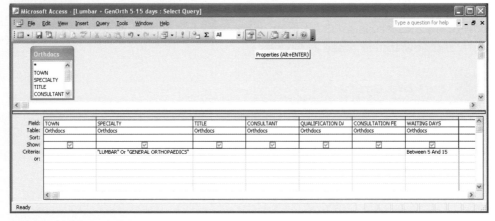

FIGURE 3.43 The query Lumbar + GenOrth 5-15 days in Design view

8 Save and close the query.

1 In your database table **Orthdocs**, create a new query.

2 Using **range** criteria, find all the consultants whose CONSULTATION FEE is **less than or equal to £140** (remember, you should not enter the currency symbol in the query criteria).

3 Using **logical** criteria, find all the consultants whose SPECIALTY is **MUSCULOSKELETAL or SPORTS INJURIES**

4 Using **wildcards**, find all the consultants whose QUALIFICATION DATE was in the **1970s**.

5 Save the query as **Sports + Musc <=140 1970s**

6 Run your query.

7 Check that the records found match the criteria you entered. The query result should display 9 records. If necessary, return to query Design view (see **How to... return to Query Design view**).

8 Your query criteria should be similar to those shown in Figure 3.44.

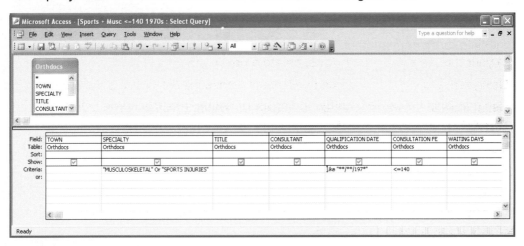

FIGURE 3.44 The query Sports + Musc <=140 1970s in Design view

9 Save and close the query.

Checking query results in Datasheet view

Once you have run your query, you should look at the records and check that those found meet the selection criteria. If you need to make changes, return to Query Design view.

▶▶ How to... *return to Query Design view*

1 With the query open in Datasheet view click on the **View** button [icon]. You will be returned to Query Design view. Make any changes to the query criteria.

2 To return to Datasheet view, click on the **View** button [icon] again or click the **Run** icon [icon].

▶▶ How to... *save an existing query*

Click on the **File** menu, click **Save**.

Calculated fields

A calculated field is a new field with a new field name. It is created in order to carry out a calculation in an existing database. Any of the four mathematical operators can be used in a calculation. In a calculated field, a field name must be enclosed in square brackets [ ]

A calculation may be carried out by adding, subtracting, multiplying or dividing one field to/by/from another.

e.g. DISCOUNT: [QUANTITY]-[SALES]

A calculation may also be carried out by adding, subtracting, multiplying or dividing one field by a figure or a percentage. Note percentages must be entered in decimal format (e.g. 25% would be entered as 0.25)

e.g. DISCOUNT: [QUANTITY]*0.1

▶▶ How to... *create a calculated field using two fields in a database table*

Calculations in databases are carried out in a Query Design view.

1 In Query Design view, drag all the fields to the Query grid.

2 Scroll to the right of all the existing fields and click in the **Field** row of the first blank field.

3 Enter the new field name, followed by a colon **:**

Then enter a square opening bracket **[**

4 Enter the existing field name exactly as it appears in the database table.

5 Enter a square closing bracket **]** then enter the appropriate mathematical operator, enter a square opening bracket **[**, then enter the second field name and a square closing bracket **]**

6 Run the query to check the results of the calculation.

> **TIP!**
>
> Ensure that you enter the field name with one hundred per cent accuracy.

Check your understanding *Create a calculated field*

1 In your database table **Orthdocs** create a new query.

2 Create a new field called **FIRST VISIT** and calculate the first visit fee by subtracting the **WAITING DAYS** from the **CONSULTATION FEE**.

3 Save the query as **INITIAL FEE**

4 Run the query.

5 Return to Query Design view and make any amendments, if required.

6 Your calculated field should be displayed as shown in Figure 3.45.

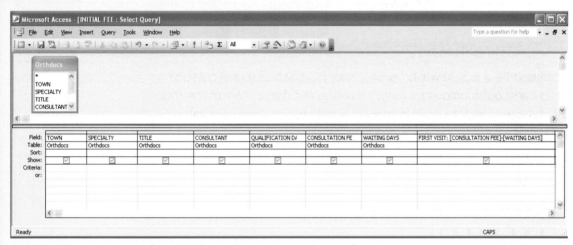

FIGURE 3.45 The query INITIAL FEE with a calculated field

7 Save and close the query.

▶▶ How to... *create a calculated field using one field and a number*

1 In Query Design view, drag all the fields to the Query grid.

2 Scroll to the right of all the existing fields and click in the **Field** row of the first blank field. Enter the new field name, followed by a colon **:** then enter a square opening bracket **[**

3 Enter the existing field name exactly as it appears in the database table.

4 Enter a square closing bracket **]** and the appropriate mathematical operator.

5 Enter the number.

6 Run the query to check the results of the calculation.

TIP!

Do not enter a space before or after the mathematical operator.

TIP!

You cannot enter a number followed by a percentage sign. To calculate a percentage, enter the number in decimal format.

1 In your database **Orthdocs**, create a new query.

2 Find all the consultants whose SPECIALTY is **TRAUMA**

3 Create a new field called **WAITING** and calculate the WAITING by subtracting **2** from the WAITING DAYS.

4 Save the Query as **Trauma Priority**

5 Run the query. The query result should display 12 records.

6 Return to Query Design view and make any amendments, if required.

7 Your query criteria and calculated field should be similar to those shown in Figure 3.46.

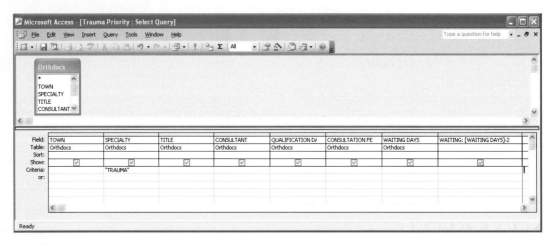

FIGURE 3.46 The query Trauma Priority with a calculated field

8 Save and close the query.

▶▶ How to... *print a query*

Before you print a query, use Print Preview to check whether all the fields and records fit on the required number of pages and check to ensure that all the data is fully displayed.

1 Click on the **File** menu, click **Print**. The **Print** dialogue box will be displayed.

2 Click on **OK**.

▶▶ How to... *close a query*

Click on the **File** menu, click **Close**.

TIP!

Always check your printout to ensure that all the data is fully displayed.

TIP!

A quick way to print is to click on the **Print** icon on the toolbar.

ASSESS YOUR SKILLS – Create queries

By working through Section 4 you will have learnt the skills listed below. Read each item to help you decide how confident you feel about each skill:

- understand range criteria, logical operators and wildcards
- understand comparison operators
- create a new query
- select field names and drag them into the Query grid
- display selected fields
- sort data in a query
- enter the selection criteria
- run the query
- create a query using two criteria
- save a new query with a specified name
- return to Query Design view
- save an existing query
- create a calculated field.

If you think you that need more practice on any of the skills in the above list, go back and work through the skill(s) again.

If you feel confident, move on to Section 5

In this section you will learn how to:

- open a saved query
- create a grouped report
- understand the parts of a grouped report
- sort data in a grouped report
- delete unwanted labels
- edit existing labels
- create a new label
- add automatic fields
- adjust the width of a report
- select control boxes
- move controls in a report
- widen a field
- change the margins
- change the font size
- change the font type
- format numeric data
- fit a report to a specified number of pages.

Reports

Reports can be based on a database table or a query. You will create reports based on queries. To create a report based on a table, use the same method.

▶▶ How to... *open a saved query*

1 In the **Database window**, in the **Objects** section, click on **Queries**. The saved queries in your database will display on the right.

2 Double-click on the query name to open the saved query.

▶▶ How to... *create a grouped report*

Records in a report can be grouped so that records containing the same information in a field (e.g. TOWN) can be displayed together. Data can then be sorted within the grouped records. Another advantage of a grouped report is that summaries can be displayed for each group (e.g.

the total, average, minimum or maximum figures in each group). Labels describing what the summaries are can be displayed automatically, or custom labels can be entered.

You will create a report using the Report Wizard. Access will open a series of Report Wizard windows.

1 With the query open in Datasheet view, click on the drop-down arrow next to the **New Object:** icon ![icon].

2 A menu will be displayed. Click on **Report**. The **New Report** dialogue box will be displayed. Click on **Report Wizard**, click **OK** (Figure 3.47). The **Report Wizard** will open.

FIGURE 3.47 The New Report dialogue box

3 In step 1 of the Report Wizard (Figure 3.48), in the **Available Fields** section, double-click on each of the field headings to be displayed in the report. Any fields you double-click will be displayed in the **Selected Fields** section (Figure 3.49).

4 Ensure that you select the fields in the order specified for the report, not in the order the fields are displayed in the list. If you select an incorrect field, click on the **Remove** button ![<]. Click on **Next**.

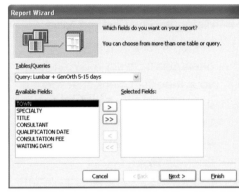

FIGURE 3.48 Step 1 of the Report Wizard

TIP!

Another method of selecting a field is to click on the field name, then click on the **Add** button ![>].To select all the fields, click on the **Add All** button ![>>].)

5 In step 2 of the Report Wizard, in the left section, select the field(s) to be grouped. Double-click or click on the **Add** button. Check that the field you have selected to be grouped on is displayed in the preview on the right of the window (Figure 3.50). Click on **Next**.

6 In step 3 (Figure 3.51), do *not* select any fields to be sorted. You will sort the fields in Design view later.

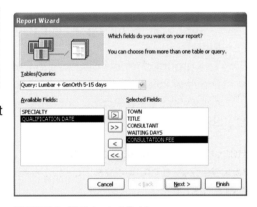

FIGURE 3.49 Selected Fields

TIP!

If you sort at this stage, Access will display the sorted field(s) as the first field(s). Changing the field order in Design view is time consuming.

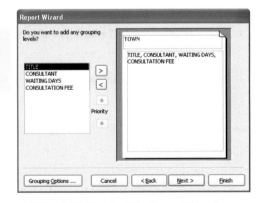

FIGURE 3.50 Step 2 of the Report Wizard

7 Click on the **Summary Options** button. The **Summary Options** dialogue box will be displayed (Figure 3.52). Only the selected fields containing numeric data will be displayed in this dialogue box. In the field row for the relevant field, click in the relevant check box.

- To display a **total**, click on **Sum**.
- To display an **average**, click on **Avg**.
- To display the **minimum number**, click on **Min**.
- To display the **maximum number**, click on **Max**.

8 Check that the option for **Detail and Summary** is selected. Click on **OK** to close the Summary Options dialogue box. Click on **Next**.

9 In step 4, select the required orientation. Select a layout for your reports. Check that there is a tick in the box for **Adjust the field width so all fields fit on a page** (Figure 3.53).

TIP!

Select the **Stepped** layout for grouped reports.

10 Click on **Next**.

11 In step 5, select a style for the report (Figure 3.54).

TIP!

Select the **Compact** style.

12 Click on **Next**.

13 In step 6, enter the report title (Figure 3.55). Click on **Finish**.

The grouped report displays in Print Preview. In Print Preview, click on the **Multiple Pages** icon and select the **2 x 3 Pages** option to see how many pages the report fits on.

Zoom in to various parts of the report (the title, field headings, records) to check if any data is not displayed in full. Make a note of any changes that need to be made.

14 Click the view icon ▾ to go to the Report Design view.

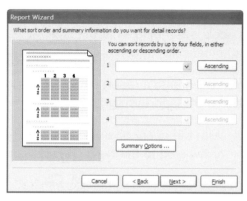

FIGURE 3.51 Step 3 of the Report Wizard

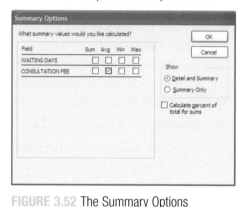

FIGURE 3.52 The Summary Options dialogue box

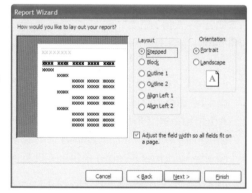

FIGURE 3.53 Step 4 of the Report Wizard

FIGURE 3.54 Step 5 of the Report Wizard

FIGURE 3.55 Step 6 of the Report Wizard

1 Open your saved query **Lumbar + GenOrth 5-15 days**.

2 Create a grouped report to display the following fields in the following order: **TOWN**, **TITLE**, **CONSULTANT**, **WAITING DAYS**, **CONSULTATION FEE**.

3 Group the report by **TOWN**.

4 Display the **AVERAGE** CONSULTATION FEE for each group.

5 Set the orientation to **portrait**.

6 Title the report **ORTHOPAEDIC CONSULTANTS**

7 Save the report using the filename **ORTHOPAEDIC CONSULTANTS**

Understanding the parts of a grouped report in Design view

Figure 3.56 shows the various parts of a grouped report in Design view.

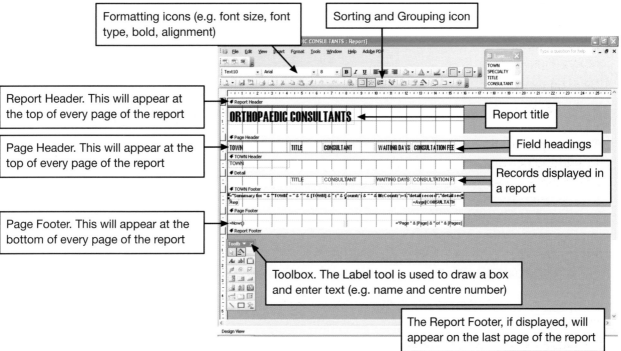

FIGURE 3.56 The parts of a grouped report in Design view

▶▶ *How to...* sort data in a grouped report

1 Click on the **View** icon to switch to Design view (if required).

2 Click on the **Sorting and Grouping** icon. The **Sorting and Grouping** dialogue box will be displayed (Figure 3.57). The field heading for the grouped field(s) will be displayed in the top row(s) of the **Field/Expression** column on the left. Do not make any changes to these fields.

TIP!

You will undo the grouping if you make any changes to the existing fields.

3 Click in the first blank row below the existing field heading(s). A drop-down arrow will be displayed in this row. From the list of fields displayed, click on the field name of the field to be sorted. The field heading will be displayed in the row.

4 Click in the same row of the field you selected in the second column for **Sort Order**.

5 Click on the drop-down arrow. Select **Ascending** or **Descending**.

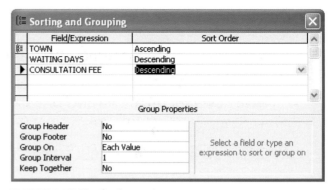

FIGURE 3.57 The Sorting and Grouping dialogue box

6 Repeat this process if you need to sort on a second field.

7 Click on the cross to close the dialogue box. The records will be sorted.

8 Switch to Print Preview to check.

Check your understanding *Sort data in a grouped report*

In your report entitled **ORTHOPAEDIC CONSULTANTS**, sort the report in descending order of **WAITING DAYS**, then in descending order of **CONSULTATION FEE**.

Making amendments to a report in Design view

▶▶ How to... *delete unwanted detail*

1 Click on the detail box. Ensure that square handles are displayed around the detail box (control) (Figure 3.58).

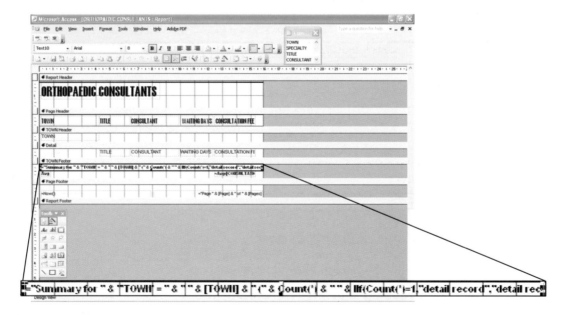

FIGURE 3.58 Deleting unwanted details

2 Press the **Delete** key.

In your report titled **ORTHOPAEDIC CONSULTANTS**, delete the whole of the following label from the **TOWN** footer area:

="Summary for " & "'TOWN' = " & " " & [TOWN] & " (" & Count(*) & " " & Iif(Count(*)=1,"detail record","detail records") & ")"

Ensure that you delete the entire control box, not just the contents.

▶▶ How to... *edit existing labels*

1 Click in the label. A warning icon may be displayed. Click on the drop-down arrow next to the warning icon and select **Ignore Error**.

2 Increase the width of the existing label control by dragging the handle to the right.

3 Click in the label box (not in the box showing the formula =…). The cursor will display.

4 Delete the existing text.

5 Enter the required label (Figure 3.59).

> **TIP!**
>
> Use Print Preview to check the new label is displayed correctly.

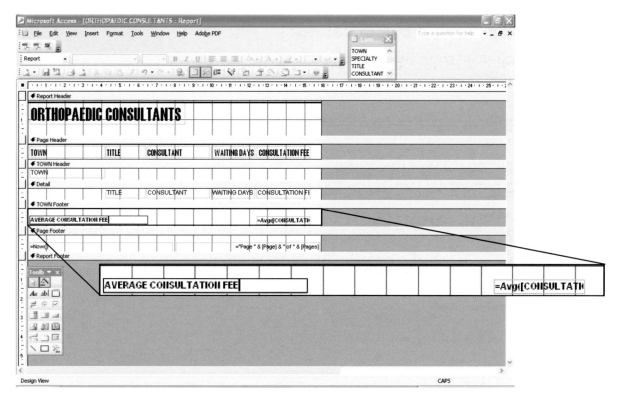

FIGURE 3.59 Entering the label

In the your report titled **ORTHOPAEDIC CONSULTANTS**, edit the existing label **Avg** to be **AVERAGE CONSULTATION FEE**

▶▶ How to... *create a new label*

1 Click and drag the grey bar below the **Page Footer** area to increase the depth of the footer area.

2 To display the Toolbox, click on the **View** menu, click on **Toolbox**.

3 From the Toolbox, select the **Label** icon.

4 Draw a text box in the **Page Footer** area. Type the required information in the text box.

5 Use Print Preview to ensure that all the labels fit on one page and that all the data is displayed in full.

▶▶ How to... *add automatic fields*

Access automatically displays the date and page number on every report. These can be moved if required or, if deleted, can be inserted again.

To insert page numbers:

1 Click on the **Insert** menu, click on **Page Numbers**.

2 Click on the drop-down arrow under **Alignment** to choose the required alignment, if required.

To add an automatic date:

1 Click on the **Insert** menu, click on **Date and Time**. The **Date and Time** dialogue box will be displayed.

2 Click on the button to choose a date format.

3 Click on **OK**.

In the footer of your report titled **ORTHOPAEDIC CONSULTANTS**, display:

An automatic date
Automatic page numbers
Your name
Your centre number

▶▶ How to... _adjust the width of a report_

1 Position the cursor at the edge of the right-hand side of the report and click. The cursor will change to a double-headed arrow ⟷.

2 Click and drag the arrow to the right to increase the width or to the left to decrease the width.

▶▶ How to... _select control boxes_

1 Click once on the control for the first control box. Square handles will be displayed around the box.

2 Hold down the **Shift** key and click on any other control box(es). Square handles will be displayed around the control boxes.

3 When you have selected the relevant fields, release the Shift key.

TIP!

Once you have made your selection, do not click on any part of the screen – you may deselect any boxes (controls) if you click.

▶▶ How to... _move controls in a report_

1 Position the cursor anywhere in the boxes you have selected. The cursor changes to a hand.

2 Click and drag the mouse to move the selected boxes. To move the control boxes very slightly press the **Ctrl** and **arrow** keys.

3 Release the mouse.

TIP!

The field order in a report can be moved by selecting the control box for the field heading and the field content as described in How to... move controls in a report.

Check your understanding _Move controls in a report_

1 In your report titled **ORTHOPAEDIC CONSULTANTS**, in the **TOWN** footer area, move all the control boxes further up in the TOWN footer section so that there is no unwanted space in this section. Ensure that you drag the grey bar up to reduce the white space.

2 Move the control boxes for the field headings and field details for **WAITING DAYS** and **CONSULTATION FEE** further to the right.

3 Move the control box for the **Avg([CONSULTATION FEE])** so that the figure is aligned in the column.

4 Save your report.

▶▶ How to... _widen a field_

1 Select the relevant field heading(s) and the field detail for each field heading selected using the method described in How to... select control boxes.

2 Drag the arrow to the right. Both the field heading and the content (the records) will be widened.

3 Use Print Preview to ensure that all the data is fully displayed.

4 If necessary, switch to Design view and make any further amendments.

1 In your report titled **ORTHOPAEDIC CONSULTANTS**, widen the field heading and field detail control boxes for the **CONSULTANT** field.

2 Adjust any other field widths as required.

3 Use Print Preview to ensure that the names of all the consultants and all data are fully displayed.

Formatting a report in Design view

▶▶ How to... *change the margins*

1 Click on the **File** menu, click on **Page Setup**, click the **Margins** tab (Figure 3.60).

2 Change the top, bottom, left and right margins as required.

3 Click on **OK**.

TIP!

Use Print Preview to check that the data now fits on the required number of pages.

FIGURE 3.60 Changing the margins

In your report titled **ORTHOPAEDIC CONSULTANTS**, change the margins in your report as follows:

Top and bottom margins **25 mm**

Left and right margins   **15 mm**

▶▶ How to... *change the font size*

TIP!

To select more than one control box, use the **Shift** key.

1 Select the control box. Ensure that square handles are displayed around the control.

2 Once you have selected the required controls, click on the drop-down arrow next to **Font Size**. From the drop-down list, select the required font size.

TIP!

Use Print Preview to check the new font size.

In your report titled **ORTHOPAEDIC CONSULTANTS**, change the font size for your name and centre number to **9**.

1 Select the control box. Ensure that square handles are displayed around the control.

2 Once you have selected the required controls, click on the drop-down arrow next to **Font Name**.

3 From the drop-down list, select the required font type.

Use Print Preview to check the new font type. Ensure that all the text is clearly legible. The emphasis (bold, italics) can be changed by clicking on the relevant icon on the Formatting toolbar.

To select more than one control box, use the **Shift** key.

To display a font name quickly, enter the first few letters of the font name in the **Font** box.

Check your understanding *Change the font type of a label in a report*

In your report titled **ORTHOPAEDIC CONSULTANTS**, change the font type for your name and centre number to **Arial**.

▶▶ **How to...** *format numeric data*

1 Click in the control box which holds the numeric value (not the label for that value).

2 Ensure that square handles are displayed around the control.

3 Right-click in the control box. A menu will be displayed. Select **Properties** (Figure 3.61). The **Text Box** dialogue box will be displayed (Figure 3.62).

4 Select the **Format** tab.

5 Click in the **Format** row. A drop-down arrow will be displayed. Click on the arrow to view the list of available formats.

If you are unsure which box it is, click on the control and press **F1**.

You may need to scroll down the list.

Do not choose the **General** option.

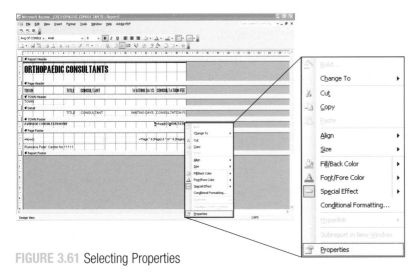

FIGURE 3.61 Selecting Properties

FIGURE 3.62 The Text Box dialogue box

6 Click on the required format.

7 Click in the **Decimal Places** row.

8 Select the number of decimal places required.

9 Click on the cross to close the Text Box dialogue box.

TIP!

To display numbers to a set number of decimal places the **Format** must be set to **Fixed** or **Currency**.

TIP!

Use Print Preview to view your report. Click on the **Multiple Pages** icon and select **2 x 3 Pages** to view all the pages. Make a note of any changes that need to be made. Click on the **View** icon to return to Design view and then make any further adjustments. Remember to use Print Preview again before printing.

Check your understanding *Format numeric data in a report*

In your report titled **ORTHOPAEDIC CONSULTANTS**, format the figure for the **AVERAGE CONSULTATION FEE** to currency with two decimal places.

▶▶ *How to...* *fit a report to a specified number of pages*

In Access there is no setting to fit to a specified number of pages. In Design view, use the following techniques to fit a report as required.

TIP!

Use Print Preview after making each amendment.

1 Change the margins.

2 Change the font size of various controls (e.g. report title, field headings, labels).

3 Change the depth of various parts of the report (e.g. report title, labels).

Check your understanding *Fit a report to a specified number of pages*

1 Ensure that the report titled **ORTHOPAEDIC CONSULTANTS** fits on to two pages.

2 Save your report.

3 Print your report. Check that all the data is fully displayed.

4 Close the report.

ASSESS YOUR SKILLS – Create a grouped report and format a report

By working through Section 5 you will have learnt the skills listed below. Read each item to help you decide how confident you feel about each skill:

- ○ open a saved query
- ○ create a grouped report
- ○ understand the parts of a general report
- ○ sort data in a grouped report
- ○ delete unwanted labels
- ○ edit existing labels
- ○ create a new label
- ○ add automatic fields
- ○ adjust the width of a report
- ○ select control boxes
- ○ move controls in a report
- ○ widen a field
- ○ change the margins
- ○ change the font size
- ○ change the font type
- ○ format numeric data
- ○ fit a report to a specified number of pages

If you think that you need more practice on any of the skills in the above list, go back and work through the skill(s) again.

If you feel confident, move on to Section 6.

6: Create a columnar and a tabular report

LEARNING OUTCOMES

In this section you will learn how to:

- ○ create a columnar report
- ○ create a tabular report displaying selected fields.

A columnar report displays data in two columns. The first column displays the field headings. These headings are repeated for every record. The second column displays the actual records. Columnar reports are generally used to display a smaller number of records.

1   With the query open in Datasheet view, click on the drop-down arrow next to the **New Object: AutoForm** icon.

2   A menu will be displayed. Click on **Report**. The **New Report** dialogue box will be displayed.

3   Click on **Report Wizard**, click **OK**. The **Report Wizard** will be displayed.

4   In the **Available Fields** section, double-click on each of the field headings to be displayed in the report. Any fields you double-click will be displayed in the **Selected Fields** section.

5   Ensure that you select the fields in the order specified for the report, not in the order the fields are displayed in the list. If you select an incorrect field, click on the **Remove** button $\boxed{<}$.

6   Click on **Next**. In step 2, Click on **Next**.

7   In step 3, do *not* select any fields to be sorted. You will sort the fields in Design view later. Click on **Next**.

8   In step 4, in the Layout section, click on **Columnar**. Select the required orientation (Figure 3.63). Click on **Next**.

9   In step 5, select a style for the report.

10 Click on **Next**.

11 In step 6, enter the Report title. Click on **Finish**. The columnar report will be displayed in Print Preview. In Print Preview, click on the **Multiple Pages** icon ▦ to check how many pages the report fits on. Zoom in to various parts of the report (the title, field headings, records) to check if any data is not displayed in full. Make a note of any changes that need to be made.

TIP!

If you have used this icon already, it converts to **New Object: Report** ▾

TIP!

Another method of selecting the available fields is to click on the field name, then click on the **Add** button $\boxed{>}$. To select all fields, click on the **Add All** button $\boxed{>>}$.

TIP!

Select the **Compact style**.

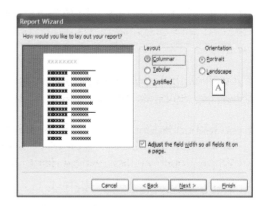

FIGURE 3.63 Step 4 of the Report Wizard

1   Open your saved query **Trauma Priority**.

2   Create a columnar report in portrait orientation to display the following fields in the following order: **TOWN, WAITING, CONSULTATION FEE**.

3   Title the report **WAITING PERIOD FOR TRAUMA PATIENTS**

4   Sort the report in ascending order of **WAITING**.

5   Left align all the control boxes for all three fields.

6   In the footer, display only your **name, centre number** and the **date**.

7   Fit the report to one page.

8   Save the report using the filename **WAITING PERIOD FOR TRAUMA PATIENTS**

9   Print your report. Check that all the data is fully displayed.

10 Close the report.

▶▶ How to...   *create a tabular report displaying selected fields*

In Section 2 you learnt how to create a tabular AutoReport to display all the fields. You will now learn how to create a tabular report that displays selected fields by using the wizard.

AutoReports apply limited formatting to a report whereas the Report Wizard allows you more flexibility when creating reports. Tabular reports display data in columns with the field headings displayed at the top of each column. Field headings are displayed at the top of every page of a report.

1   With the query open in Datasheet view, click on the drop-down arrow next to the **New Object:** icon.

2   A menu will be displayed. Click on **Report**. The **New Report** dialogue box will be displayed. Click on **Report Wizard**, click **OK**. The **Report Wizard** dialogue box will be displayed.

3   In the **Available Fields** section, double-click on each of the field headings to be displayed in the report. Any fields you double-click will be displayed in the **Selected Fields** section.

4   Ensure that you select the fields in the order specified for the report, not in the order the fields are displayed in the list. If you select an incorrect field, click on the **Remove** button 〔 < 〕. Click on **Next**.

5   In step 2, click on **Next**.

6   In step 3, do not select any fields to be sorted. You will sort the fields in Design view later. Click on **Next**.

7   In step 4, click on the button to select **Tabular**. Select the orientation. Click on **Next**.

TIP!

Select the **Compact style**.

8   In step 5, select a style for the report.

9   Click on **Next**.

10 In step 6, enter the Report title. Click on **Finish**. The tabular report displays in Print Preview. In Print Preview, click on the **Multiple Pages** icon to see how many pages the report fits on. Zoom in to various parts of the report (the title, field headings, records) to check if any data is not displayed in full. Make a note of any changes that need to be made.

Check your understanding *Create a tabular report using the Report Wizard*

1   Open your saved query **Sports + Musc <=140 1970s**.

2   Create a tabular report displaying the following fields in the following order:

SPECIALTY
WAITING DAYS
TITLE
CONSULTANT
TOWN

3   Set the orientation to **landscape**.

4   Enter the report title **SPORTS INJURIES EXPERIENCED CONSULTANTS**

5   Sort the report in descending order of **QUALIFICATION DATE**.

6   In the footer, enter your name. Make sure the date is displayed. Do not display the page number.

7   Make sure that all the data is fully displayed.

8   Save the report using the name **SPORTS INJURIES EXPERIENCED CONSULTANTS**

9   Print the report.

10 Close the report.

11 Close any open tables or queries and exit Access.

ASSESS YOUR SKILLS – Create a columnar and a tabular report

By working through Section 6 you will have learnt the skills listed below. Read each item to help you decide how confident you feel about each skill:

○ create a columnar report

○ create a tabular report displaying selected fields.

If you think that you need more practice on any of the skills in the above list, go back and work through the skill(s) again.

If you feel confident, do the Build-up and Practice tasks on page 66.

QUICK REFERENCE – *Create a new database, create a tabular report and labels*

Keep a copy of this page next to you. Refer to it when working through tasks and during any assessments.

Click means click with the left mouse button

HOW TO	METHOD
Create a new blank database	Load Microsoft Access 2003 → click on the File menu, New → the task pane is displayed on the right → click on Blank Database → the File New Database dialogue box will be displayed → click on the drop-down arrow next to Save in and go to your user area → in the File Name box delete db1 and type in an appropriate filename → click on Create → the Database window will be displayed → check that Tables is selected in the Objects section on the left → on the right, double-click on Create table in Design view → Table Design view will be displayed.
Enter field names, set the data type and the field properties	In Table Design view, check that the cursor is in the first Field Name row → enter the first field heading in the Field Name column → press the Tab key to move to the Data Type column (or click in the Data Type column) → click on the drop-down arrow to select the data type → in the Field Properties section set the properties → click in the second row in the Field Name column and repeat the process for all remaining fields.
Save and name the table	Click on the Save icon → the Save As dialogue box will be displayed → type in the table name → click on OK → Access will display a message asking you if you want to create a primary key → click on No → click on the View icon to switch to Datasheet view.
Enter records	In Datasheet view check that the cursor is flashing in the first field → enter the required data → press the Tab key to move to the next field and enter the data → to place a tick in a logic field box, click in the box with your mouse or press the spacebar → in numeric and currency fields, enter the data (the zeros will be overtyped) → press the Tab key to move to the next record
Widen a field	Position the cursor on the line to the right of the field heading → the cursor will turn into a double-headed arrow → double-click → Access will adjust the column width to fit the longest line of data on the screen within the field.
Create an AutoReport	With the table/query open in Datasheet view (as a table), click on the drop-down arrow next to New Object:→ a menu will be displayed → click on Report → the New Report dialogue box will be displayed → click on AutoReport: Tabular → OK.
Switch to report Design view	Click on the View icon → the report will display in Design view.

HOW TO	METHOD
Sort data	In Design view, click on the Sorting and Grouping icon → the Sorting and Grouping dialogue box will be displayed → the cursor will be displayed in the first row of the Field/Expression column → click on the drop-down arrow in this row → a list of field headings will be displayed → select the field to be sorted → in the Sort Order column, click on the drop-down arrow and select Ascending or Descending → click on the cross to close the Sorting and Grouping dialogue box.
Delete the page number or date	In Design view, click once in the box for the page numbers → square handles will be displayed around the control box → press the Delete key (the date can be deleted using the same method).
Insert name and centre number	In Design view, click on the View menu, Page Header/Footer → to display the Toolbox, click on the View menu, Toolbox → from the Toolbox, select the Label icon → draw a text box in the page footer area → type the information in the text box.
Set the page orientation	Click on the File menu → Page Setup → Page tab → select Portrait or Landscape.
Change the margins	In the Page Setup window, click on the Margins tab → change the top, bottom, left and right margins → click on OK.
Widen the report title control box and enter a report title	In Report Design view, click on the report title → square handles will be displayed around the control box → click and drag the square handle on the right of the control box further to the right to widen the control → click in the box for the report title → a cursor will be displayed → delete the existing title and enter the new title.
Save a report with a specified name	Click on the File menu, Save → the Save As dialogue box will be displayed → delete the existing name and enter the report name → click on OK.
Close a report	Click on the File menu → Close.
Open a saved table	In the Database window, in the Objects section, click on Tables → the tables in your database will be displayed → double-click on the table name to open it.
Create labels	In table Datasheet view, click on the drop-down arrow next to New Object: AutoForm → click on Report → the New Report dialogue box will be displayed → click on Label Wizard, OK → the Label Wizard will be displayed → select the label dimensions and manufacturer → click on Next → in step 2 select the font name and font size → click on Next → in step 3 double-click in turn on each of the Field Headings required → to display two fields on one line press the space bar between two fields → press Enter to display the next field on a new line → click on Next → in step 4 double-click on the field(s) to be sorted → click on Next → in step 5 enter the name of the label report → click on Finish → to display headers and footers, switch to label report Design view.
Display headers and footers on a label report	In Design view, click on the View menu, Page Header/Footer, then click on the View menu again, Page Header/Footer (or if page headers and footers are already displayed, drag the grey bar to an appropriate height for the header and footer) → click on the View menu, Toolbox → from the Toolbox, select the Label icon → draw a text box in the page footer area (or header area) → type the information in the text box.

Click means click with the left mouse button

QUICK REFERENCE – Import a csv file, update a database, create queries and create a report

Keep a copy of this page next to you. Refer to it when working through tasks and during any assessments.

HOW TO	METHOD
Import a csv file	Load Access → create a new blank database → click on the File menu, Get External Data, Import → click on the drop-down arrow next to Look in → go to the user area where the csv file is saved → click on the drop-down arrow to the right of Files of type → select Text Files → in the Look in box click on the csv file to be imported → ensure the filename is highlighted → click on Import → in step 1 ensure the Delimited option is selected → click on Next → in step 2 ensure the Comma option is selected → click on the drop-down arrow to the right of Text Qualifier → select " (double speech marks) → click in the check box for First Row Contains Field Names → click on Next → in step 3 check that the option for In a New Table is selected → click on Next → in step 4 click on Next → in step 5 click the button for No Primary Key → click on Next → in step 6 click on Finish → in step 7 you should see the message Finished importing file... → click on OK.
Modify the field characteristics	Switch to Table Design view → click in the Data Type column of the field to be modified → in the Field Properties section amend the properties → repeat for all other the fields → click on the Save icon.
Add a new record	Click on the New Record icon in the Record Navigation buttons or click in first column of a blank row → enter the new data → use the Tab key to move from field to field and to move to the next record.
Find a record in a large database and delete it	Click anywhere in the relevant field → click on the Edit menu, Find → the Find and Replace dialogue box will be displayed → in the Find What box enter the data → click on the drop-down arrow next to Match → select the option for Any Part of Field → click on the Find Next button → close the Find and Replace dialogue box → ensure the cursor is displayed in the record to be deleted → click on the Edit menu, Delete Record → Access will display a message prompting you to confirm the delete → click on Yes.
Amend existing data	Click in the field (cell) to be replaced → delete the unwanted data → enter the new data.
Replace data	Click anywhere in the relevant field (column) → click on the Edit menu, Replace → the Find and Replace dialogue box will be displayed → in the Find What box, enter the data to be replaced → in the Replace With box, enter the new data (the code) → check that the Match box displays Whole Field or Any Part of Field (as required) → click to place a tick in the Match Case box → click on Replace All → Access will display a message asking you to confirm the replace → click on Yes → click on the cross to close the Find and Replace dialogue box.
Delete a field	Switch to table Design view → click in the row in the field to be deleted (click in the Field Name or Data Type column) → click on the Edit menu, Delete Rows → Access will displays a message prompting you to confirm the delete → click on Yes.

HOW TO	METHOD
Go to Query Design view	*Method 1 (quicker method)* With the database table open, click on the drop-down arrow next to the New Object: icon → a drop-down menu will be displayed → click on Query → the New Query dialogue box will be displayed → check that Design view is selected → click on OK. *Method 2* Close the table → in the Database window, click on Queries in the Objects section → click on Create query in Design view, Open → the Show Table Dialogue box will be displayed → click to select the table name → click on Add, Close.
Select all fields to place them in the Query grid	Double-click on the table name in the Field List box in the top section of Query Design view → all field headings (field names) will be highlighted → position the cursor in the highlighted field names → click and drag the field names to the Query grid → release the mouse button in the field row of the first column → all the field headings will be placed in separate columns.
Select certain fields and place them in the Query grid	In the Field List box, double-click on each field name (field heading) required → each field will be placed in the Query grid.
Enter the selection criteria	Click in the Criteria row of the field to be queried → enter the required criteria.
Enter comparison operators for numbers	> more than >= more than and equal to < less than <= less than and equal to between between a range of numbers
Enter comparison operators for dates	> after >= after or on < before <= before or on between between a range of dates
Enter selection criteria in two fields	In the Query grid, click in the Criteria row of the field to be queried → enter the criterion → click in the next field → enter the criterion.
Sort data in queries	Click in the Sort row of the field to be sorted → a drop-down arrow will be displayed → click on the drop-down arrow → select Ascending or Descending.

HOW TO	METHOD
Display selected fields	Click in the Show box to remove the tick for the fields (columns) that should not be displayed.
Run a query	Click on the Run icon in Design view → the results of the query will be displayed as a table in Datasheet view → the number of records found are displayed in the Record Navigation buttons at the bottom left of Datasheet view.
Save a query with a specified name	Click on the File menu, Save → the Save As dialogue box will be displayed → delete the text Query1 → enter the query name → click on OK.
Return to Query Design view to make amendments	Click on the View button → make the changes in the Query grid → click on Run to run the query.
Save an existing query	Click on the File menu, Save.
Prepare to print a query	Click on Print Preview → use Zoom to zoom in to different parts of the table → check the longest line in each column is fully displayed → check that all the fields (columns) fit on one page → click on the Close button to close Print Preview → make any changes to the layout in Datasheet view → use Print Preview again (change the orientation if required – see Set the page orientation).
Print a query	Click on the File menu, Print → in the Print dialogue box, click on OK (or click on the Print icon).
Close a query	Click the File menu →click Close.
Create a calculated field using two fields in a database table	In Query Design view, drag all the fields to the Query grid → scroll to the right of all the existing fields and click in the Field row of the first blank field → enter the new field name followed by a colon : → enter a square opening bracket [→ enter the existing field name exactly as it appears in the database table → enter a square closing bracket]→ enter the appropriate mathematical operator → enter a square opening bracket → enter the second field name → enter a square closing bracket → run the query to check the results of the calculation.
Create a calculated field using one field and a number	In Query Design view, drag all the fields to the Query grid → scroll to the right of all the existing fields and click in the Field row of the first blank field → enter the new field name followed by a colon : → enter a square opening bracket [→ enter the existing field name exactly as it appears in the database table → enter a square closing bracket] → enter the appropriate mathematical operator (do not enter a space before or after the mathematical operator) → enter the number (to calculate a percentage, enter the number in decimal format) → run the query to check the results of the calculation.
Open a saved query	In the Database window, in the Objects section, click on Tables → the saved queries in the database will be displayed on the right → double-click on the query name to open it.

HOW TO	METHOD
Create a grouped report	Open the query in Datasheet view → click on the drop-down arrow next to the New Object icon → a menu will be displayed → click on Report → the New Report dialogue box will be displayed → click on Report Wizard, OK → the Report Wizard will be displayed → in the Available Fields section, double-click on the field headings in the order they need to appear in the report → click on Next → in step 2, in the left section, select the field(s) to be grouped → double-click → click on Next → in step 3 do *not* select any fields to be sorted → click on the Summary Options button → the Summary Options dialogue box will be displayed → in the field row for the relevant field, click in the relevant check box → check that the option for Detail and Summary is selected → click on OK → click on Next in the Report Wizard box → in step 4 select the required orientation → select a layout → check there is a tick in the box for Adjust the field width so all fields fit on a page → click on Next → in step 5 select a style → click on Next → in step 6 enter the report title → click on Finish.
Sort data in a grouped report	Click on the View icon to switch to report Design view → click on the Sorting and Grouping icon → the Sorting and Grouping dialogue box will be displayed → the field heading for the grouped field(s) will be displayed in the top row(s) of the Field/Expression column on the left (do not make any changes to these fields) → click in the first blank row below the existing field heading(s) → a drop-down arrow will be displayed in this row → click on the drop-down arrow and select the field name of the field to be sorted → the field heading will be displayed in this row → click in the same row of the field you selected in the second column for Sort Order → click on the drop-down arrow and select Ascending or Descending → repeat this process if you need to sort on a second field → click on the cross to close the window.
Delete unwanted labels	Click on the label → ensure that square handles are displayed around the label box (control) → press the Delete key.
Edit existing labels	Click in the label → a cursor will be displayed in the control box → a warning tag may display → click on the drop-down arrow next to the warning icon and select Ignore Error → increase the width of the existing label control by dragging the handle to the right → click in the label box → delete the existing text → enter the label.
Create a new label	Click and drag the report footer section to increase the depth of the page footer → to display the Toolbox, click on the View menu, Toolbox → from the Toolbox, select the Label icon → click and drag the grey bar below the page footer area to increase the depth of the footer area → draw a text box in the page footer area → type the information in the text box.
Adjust the width of a report	Position the cursor at the edge of the right-hand side of the report and click → the cursor will change to a double-headed arrow → click and drag the arrow to the right to increase the width or to the left to decrease the width.
Select control boxes	Click once on the control for the first control box → square handles will be displayed around the box → hold down the Shift key and click on any other control box(es) → square handles will be displayed around the control boxes → when you have selected the relevant fields, let go of the Shift key.

HOW TO	METHOD
Move controls in a report	Position the cursor anywhere in the boxes that you selected → the cursor changes to a hand symbol → click and drag the hand symbol to move the selected boxes → release the mouse.
Widen a field	Select the relevant field heading(s) and the field detail for each field heading selected using the method described above → drag the arrow to the right → both the field heading and the content (the records) will be widened.
Add automatic fields	*Note:* Access automatically displays the date and page number on every report. Therefore you may not need to insert the date and page number. To insert page numbers, click on the Insert menu, Page Numbers → to add an automatic date, click on the Insert menu, Date and Time → the Date and Time dialogue box will be displayed → choose a date format → click on OK.

Click means click with the left mouse button

QUICK REFERENCE – *Format a report in Design view, create a columnar and a tabular report*

Keep a copy of this page next to you. Refer to it when working through tasks and during any assessments.

HOW TO	METHOD
Change the margins	Click on the File menu, Page Setup, Margins tab → change the margins as required → click on OK.
Change the font size	Select the control box → ensure that square handles are displayed around the control box → to select more than one control box use the Shift key → click on the drop-down arrow next to the Font Size box → from the drop-down list, select the font size.
Change the font type	Select the control box → ensure that square handles are displayed around the control box → click on the drop-down arrow next to the Font Name box → from the drop-down list, select the font type.
Format numeric data	Click on the control box which holds the numeric value (not the label for that value) → ensure that square handles are displayed around the control box → right-click in the control box → a menu will be displayed → select Properties → the Text Box dialogue box will be displayed → select the Format tab → click in the Format row → a drop-down menu will be displayed → click on the drop-down arrow → a list of available formats will be displayed → click on the required format → click in the Decimal Places row → select the number of decimal places required → click on the cross to close the Text Box dialogue box.
Create a columnar report	Open the query in Datasheet view → click on the drop-down arrow next to the New Object icon → a menu will be displayed → click on Report → the New Report dialogue box will be displayed → click on Report Wizard, OK → the Report Wizard will be displayed → in the Available Fields section, double-click on the field headings required in the order they need to appear in the report → click on Next → in step 2 click on Next → in step 3 do *not* select any fields to be sorted → click on Next → in step 4 select Columnar → select the orientation → click on Next → in step 5 select a style → click on Next → in step 6 enter the report title → click on Finish.
Create a tabular report displaying selected fields	Open the query in Datasheet view → click on the drop-down arrow next to the New Object icon → a menu will be displayed → click on Report → the New Report dialogue box will be displayed → click on Report Wizard, OK → the Report Wizard will be displayed → in the Available Fields section, double-click on each of the field headings required → click on Next → in step 2 click on Next → in step 3 do *not* select any fields to be sorted → click on Next → in step 4 select Tabular and select the orientation → click on Next → in step 5 select a style → click on Next → in step 6 enter the report title → click on Finish.

Scenario

You work for a distribution company that specialises in selling books. You have been asked to create a small database to hold details of the company sales representatives.

1 Open a database software application.

2 Create a new database called **reps**

3 In a new table, set up the field headings and data types as shown below. Ensure that the field lengths are long enough to display all the information in full.

FIELD HEADING	DATA TYPE
FIRST NAME	Text
LAST NAME	Text
REGION	Text
HOURS	Number, 0 decimal places
PAY RATE	Currency, 2 decimal places with currency symbol
COMPANY CAR	Logic field
START DATE	English date format (day, month, year)

4 Enter the records shown below into your database table. You may use a data entry form to enter this data.

FIRST NAME	LAST NAME	REGION	HOURS	PAY RATE	COMPANY CAR	START DATE
WILLIAM	GABAR	NORTH EAST	35	16.75	YES	05/05/1970
ARTHUR	MARINO	NORTH WEST	40	16.00	YES	03/01/1983
DYLAN	JONES	WALES	20	21.50	NO	25/07/1998
VERDA	OLNICK	MIDLANDS	25	21.50	NO	06/04/2004
JASMINE	SPARGO	SOUTH EAST	35	23.75	NO	14/08/2002
DONALD	JANAI	SOUTH WEST	40	16.00	YES	26/09/1996
JANINE	WINSTON	SCOTLAND	25	16.75	YES	03/03/2000
GILL	O'SULLIVAN	IRELAND	35	16.50	YES	12/04/2005
SIMRAN	KHAN	LONDON	20	25.00	NO	01/02/1989

5 Check your data for accuracy and save the table.

BUILD-UP TASK ② Create a calculated field in a query

You have been asked to calculate the weekly wages for each of the sales representatives.

1 In a query, create a new field called **WAGE** and calculate the wage for each sales representative by multiplying the **HOURS** by the **PAY RATE**.

2 Save the query using the name **REPS PAY**

BUILD-UP TASK ③ Format and print a tabular report

1 Using the query **REPS PAY** you saved in Build-up task 2, produce a **tabular** report, in **landscape** orientation, displaying all the records.

2 Display all the fields in the following order:

FIRST NAME
LAST NAME
REGION
HOURS
PAY RATE
COMPANY CAR
START DATE
WAGE

3 Title the report **WEEKLY PAYMENTS TO SALES REPS**

4 Sort the data in descending order of **WAGE**.

5 Format the figures in the **WAGE** column to be displayed to **two** decimal places with a currency symbol.

6 Ensure the figures in the **PAY RATE** column are also displayed to **two** decimal places with a currency symbol.

7 In the footer display:

an automatic date field
your name
your centre number

> **TIP!**
> You may change the font type, size and alignment.

8 Ensure all data will be fully displayed on the printout.

9 Save the report as **WEEKLY PAYMENTS TO SALES REPS**

10 Print the report on **one** page in **landscape** orientation.

BUILD-UP TASK ④ *Create and print labels*

The sales representatives will be attending a conference. Name labels need to be printed for each of the representatives.

1   Display the following fields on the labels:

   FIRST NAME   LAST NAME (on one line, separated by at least one space)
   REGION

2   Sort the data in ascending order of **LAST NAME**.

3   Do not display field headings on the labels.

4   In the footer, display your **name** and **centre number**.

5   Ensure all the data will be fully displayed on the printout.

6   Print the labels on **one** page.

7   Save and close the database.

BUILD-UP TASK ⑤ *Import a csv file and update a database*

A datafile of books (in csv format) has been created. You have been asked to import this file into your database software and update the database. You will need the datafile **DBBOOKS**. (*Note*: some entries in the **AUTHOR** field are intentionally blank – i.e. do not contain data.)

1   Create a new database using the name **stockbks**

2   Import the csv file **DBBOOKS** and save it as a new table in your database software's file format.

3   Modify the field characteristics as shown below.

FIELD HEADING	DATA TYPE
ISBN NO	Text
TITLE	Text
AUTHOR	Text
PUBLISHER	Text
YEAR	Number, 0 decimal places
PRICE	Currency, 2 decimal places with currency symbol
DELIVERY	Text
PAGES	Number, 0 decimal places
TYPE	Text

4   You need to amend the following data. Delete the records with ISBN NO **1842242105** and AUTHOR **Hudson Bob**.

5   In the **Type** field, replace *all* the entries for **Paperback** with **PB** and **Hardback** with **HB**

6   Save the database table.

You have been asked to query the database to provide specific reports for the manager. A customer has asked for a list of books that could be recommended to students.

1 In a query, find all the titles where the **PRICE** is **£29.95 or less** and the **DELIVERY** is **STOCKED** or **1 DAY** or **2 DAYS** or **3 DAYS**.

2 Save the query as **UNDER 30 QUICK DELIVERY**

BUILD-UP TASK ⑦ Create and format a tabular grouped report

1 Use the query **UNDER 30 QUICK DELIVERY** created in Build-up task 6 to produce a tabular report in landscape orientation entitled **POSSIBLE BOOK RECOMMENDATIONS**.

2 Display the following fields in the following order: **PUBLISHER**, **ISBN NO**, **TITLE**, **DELIVERY**, **PRICE**.

3 Group the report by **PUBLISHER**

4 Sort the data in the **PUBLISHER** field in **ascending** order, then sort the data within each group in **descending** order of **PRICE**.

5 For each group, display the **Total** figure for **PRICE** and also display the **Overall Total** figure.

6 Enter the label **COST IF ORDERED FOR LIBRARY** for the figure for each group.

7 Enter the label **TOTAL COST IF ALL BOOKS RECOMMENDED** for the overall total figure.

8 Format the **PRICE** figures and all the **Total** figures to be displayed to **two** decimal places with a currency symbol.

9 Align the **Total** figures under the **PRICE** column.

10 In the footer display:

an automatic date field
automatic page numbers
your name
your centre number

11 Ensure all the data is fully visible.

12 Save the report as **POSSIBLE BOOK RECOMMENDATIONS** and print the report in **landscape** orientation to fit on no more than **three** pages.

BUILD-UP TASK ⑧ Create a query using logical, range and wildcard criteria

The manager wants to promote publications with CD-ROMS and shorter publications.

1. In a query, find all the titles where the **TYPE** includes a **CD-ROM** or is **PB** or **HB** and where the **PAGES** are between **36** and **200**.

2. Save the query as **PROMOTIONS**

BUILD-UP TASK ⑨ Create and format a columnar report

1. Use the query **PROMOTIONS** created in Build-up task 8 to produce a columnar report in portrait orientation entitled **BOOK PROMOTIONS**

2. Display the following fields in the following order: **TITLE, TYPE, PRICE**.

3. Sort the data in **ascending** order of **PRICE**.

4. In the footer display:

   your name
   your centre number

5. Ensure all the data is fully visible.

6. Save the report as **TITLES FOR PROMOTION** and print the report in **portrait** orientation to fit on no more than **one** page.

Task 1

Scenario

You work as a Customer Support Assistant in a travel agency that specialises in low-cost holidays in the sun. Your duties include the creating, updating and querying the company databases. You have been asked to create a small database of holiday representatives who are available for work during the summer season.

1 Open a database software application.

2 Create a new database called **holiday reps**

3 In a new table, set up the field headings and data types as shown below. Ensure that the field lengths are long enough to display all the information in full.

FIELD HEADING	DATA TYPE
FAMILY NAME	Text
GIVEN NAME	Text
DOB	English date format (day, month, year)
CONTACT NUMBER	Text
FIRST SEASON	Logic field
PREFERENCE	Text
WORK DAYS	Number, 0 decimal places
WEEKLY WAGE	Currency, 2 decimal places with currency symbol

4 Enter the records shown below into your database table. You may use a data entry form to enter the data.

FAMILY NAME	GIVEN NAME	DOB	CONTACT NUMBER	FIRST SEASON	PREFERENCE	WORK DAYS	WEEKLY WAGE
BRETT	SIMON	04/02/1978	0796 621 8997	YES	TURKEY TUNISIA	5	350.00
ABSOLM	JODI	30/09/1986	0203 546 1374	NO	SPAIN	6	195.75
FALLATHI	ALI	28/01/1980	0203 671 8993	NO	CYPRUS TURKEY	5	375.50
HOKER	ANGELA	14/09/1987	0530 824 4433	YES	BALERIC ISLANDS	6	225.50
SAVINE	DENISE	21/03/1986	0797 540 6213	YES	FRANCE SPAIN	5	180.00
BROOKS	SAM	05/05/1985	0204 311 7968	NO	GREECE	6	195.75
SIMMS	LISA	09/12/1986	0114 236 3800	YES	GREECE	6	195.75
PATEL	KAYUREE	11/05/1986	0771 406 3501	YES	TURKEY	4	300.75
PREET	KIRAN	27/11/1987	0797 914 6336	YES	SPAIN	6	225.50

5 Check your data for accuracy and save the table.

Task 2

1 Using the database table saved in Task 1 produce a **tabular** report, in **landscape** orientation, displaying all records.

2 Display all fields in the following order:

FAMILY NAME
GIVEN NAME
DOB
CONTACT NUMBER
FIRST SEASON
PREFERENCE
WORK DAYS
WEEKLY WAGE

3 Title the report **SUMMER SEASON HOLIDAY REPS**

4 Sort the data in **descending** order of **DOB**.

5 In the footer display:

an automatic date field
your name
your centre number

6 Ensure all the data will be fully displayed on the printout.

7 Save and print the report on **one** page in **landscape** orientation.

8 Labels for the files of each representative need to be printed. Display the following fields on the labels:

GIVEN NAME   **FAMILY NAME** (on one line, separated by at least one space)
PREFERENCE
WORK DAYS

9 Sort the data in **descending** order of **WORK DAYS** then in **ascending** order of **FAMILY NAME**.

10 Do not display field headings on the labels.

11 In the footer, display your **name** and **centre number**.

12 Ensure all the data will be fully displayed on the printout. Save the labels report.

13 Print the labels on **one** page.

14 Save and close the database.

Task 3

A datafile (in csv format) of available holidays has been created. You have been asked to query this data to provide specific reports for customers. You will need the csv file **holiday**.

1 Create a new database using the name **summer 2007**

2 Import the file **holiday** and save it as a new table in your database software's file format.

3 Modify the field characteristics as shown in the following table.

FIELD HEADING	DATA TYPE
COUNTRY	Text
STAR RATING	Number, 0 decimal places
TYPE	Text
PROPERTY	Text
SUITS	Text
COST	Currency, 0 decimal places with currency symbol
CHILD DISCOUNT	Logic
AIRPORT	Text
DATE	English date (day, month, year) in any format
DAYS	Number, 0 decimal places

4 One of the hotels has been found to be unsatisfactory. Delete the record for **Tunisia** with a STAR RATING of **2** leaving from **London Gatwick** AIRPORT.

5 The price of one holiday has been reduced. Amend the record for **France** with a STAR RATING of **4** in a **Villa** PROPERTY to have a COST of **999** instead of 1020.

6 In the **TYPE** field replace entries for:

Self Catering with **SC**
Half Board with **HB**
Full Board with **FB**
Bed and Breakfast with **BB**
All Inclusive with **AI**

7 Save the database table.

8 You have been asked to calculate the child discounts for holidays in late July where a child discount is available. In a query, find all the holidays where the **CHILD DISCOUNT** is **YES** and the **DATE** is **Between 21/07/07 and 28/07/07**.

9 In the same query, create a new field called **REDUCTION PER CHILD** and calculate the amount of the reduction by multiplying the **COST** by **40%** (COST*0.4).

10 Save the query using the name **CHILD REDUCTIONS**

Task 4

1 Use your saved query called **CHILD REDUCTIONS** to produce a **columnar** report in **portrait** orientation. Title the report **LATE JULY CHILD DISCOUNTS**

2 Display the following fields in the following order:

DATE
DAYS
COUNTRY
STAR RATING
TYPE
COST
REDUCTION PER CHILD

3 Sort the data in **descending** order of **REDUCTION PER CHILD**.

4 Format the figures in the **COST** column to be displayed to **integer** (no decimal places) with a currency symbol.

5 Format the figures in the **REDUCTION PER CHILD** column to be displayed to **integer** (no decimal places) with a currency symbol.

6 In the footer display:

an automatic date field
automatic page numbers
your name
your centre number

7 Ensure all the data is fully visible and fits on no more than **two** pages. You may alter the margins and the format of the report to achieve this.

8 Save the report as **CHILD DISCOUNTS IN JULY**

9 Print the report in **portrait** orientation to fit on no more than **two** pages.

Task 5

1 A customer has asked for a list of holidays to suit their preferences and budget. In a query, find all the holidays where the STAR RATING is **4 or more**, leaving from *any* **London** AIRPORT and the PROPERTY is a **Villa** or **Hotel** or **Resort**.

2 Save the query as **4* PLUS LONDON**

3 Use the query **4* PLUS LONDON** to produce a **tabular** report in **landscape** orientation titled **LUXURY HOLIDAYS FROM LONDON AIRPORTS**

4 Display the following fields in the following order: **COUNTRY**, **DATE**, **DAYS**, **TYPE**, **PROPERTY**, **STAR RATING**, **COST**.

5 Group the report by **COUNTRY**.

6 Sort the data in the **COUNTRY** field in **ascending** order, then sort the data within each group in **ascending** order of **DATE**.

7 For each group, display the **Minimum** figure for **COST**.

8 Enter the label **LEAST EXPENSIVE HOLIDAY** for the figure for each group.

9 Format the **COST** figures and the **Minimum** figures to be displayed as **integer** (no decimal places) with a currency symbol.

10 Align the **Minimum** figures under the **COST** column.

11 In the footer display:

   an automatic date field
   automatic page numbers
   your name
   your centre number

12 Ensure all the data is fully visible.

13 Save the report as **LUXURY HOLS FROM LONDON** and print the report in **landscape** orientation to fit on no more than **two** pages.

Amend To change or to edit.

Back up To create a spare copy.

Calculated field A new field created in Query Design view in order to carry out a calculation.

Click and drag A mouse technique used to move items. The mouse button is held down so that the cursor can be moved to reposition an item.

Codes Abbreviations that stand for longer words, often referred to as 'encoding data'. Codes help to maintain database efficiency.

Comparison operator Used in queries to search for information in numeric and date fields. Information from the database is compared with the criteria entered, and matching results are displayed.

OPERATOR	IN NUMERIC FIELDS	IN DATE FIELDS
>	more than	after
<	less than	before
>=	more than and equal to	on or after
<=	less than and equal to	on or before

Control A label or text box that controls the display of information in a report.

Criteria More than one criterion. The selection conditions used in one or more fields.

Criterion A selection condition used in a query to find specific records.

csv file 'Comma separated values' or 'comma separated variables'. A generic file format that can be opened and read by a wide range of software.

Data file A file in any file format that contains data.

Data type The type of data in a field (e.g. text, number, date, currency).

Database An organised list of information.

Database window A window that lists all the objects currently in the database. Clicking on an object in the Objects sections allows a user to view the objects in that section (e.g. tables, queries, reports).

Datasheet view View of a table or query in rows and columns showing all the data in all the records. The field names appear as column headings and the records as rows.

Decimal places The number of figures displayed after the decimal point.

Default The automatic setting(s) in Access. The setting that a computer program (or system) will use unless it is changed or 'customised'. For example, the default font for a table in Access may be Arial. Unless you change this, tables will always be displayed in this font.

Delete a record Removing the contents of a record completely. The remaining record numbers are automatically renumbered.

Design view View of a table, query or report showing how it is designed. A user can make amendments in Design view.

Field A separate item (block) of data that makes up a record.

Field heading A field name (column heading).

Field name A column heading that describes the data in that column. Referred to as a 'field heading'.

Field properties The formatting for the data type (e.g. currency with two decimal places or a field length of 25 characters for a text field).

Find and replace A technique where the computer searches for a particular word or character in a table and replaces instances of that word or character with alternative words or characters.

Folder An area created to store and organise files.

Form A display on the screen which allows a user to enter records into the table. A form may also be used for viewing data.

Formatting How data is displayed (e.g. with a currency symbol, in bold, in a particular font type or font size).

Grouped report A grouped report combines data into groups. A grouped report can include calculations such as totals, averages and maximum and minimum values.

Grouping Records with the same information in a field are displayed together.

Hover To position the cursor over an object/area on the screen.

Import To insert prepared data into an Access table.

Label A text box displaying data that will not change.

Labels This is a type of report designed to be printed on label sheets. A label report does not display a report title.

Logical operator AND, OR and NOT. Used in queries to combine search criteria.

Object An element within the database (e.g. a table, query, form or report).

Orientation The way paper is displayed. The orientation can be portrait (shortest side at the top) or landscape (widest side at the top).

Print Preview Displays on-screen what a table, query or report will look like when printed.

Query A method of questioning a database to find specific information.

Query Design view The view in which queries are created. It is divided into two sections. The top section displays a field list box which displays the table name and the field headings. The lower section is the Query grid (see *Query grid*).

Query grid The lower part of the query window where criteria are entered, data is sorted and the display of fields is selected.

Range A set of values that have a lower and upper limit.

Read only A property set on a file which does not allow the user to make any changes to the file. To amend a file, the user must remove the read-only property.

Record A set of related data. Similar to a row in a table.

Record Navigation buttons Buttons at the bottom left of the screen in Datasheet view. Allow a user to move between records in a table or query. They display the number of records in a table or query.

Report A more professional way of displaying information from a table or query.

Run (a query) Finds all the records that meet the criteria entered into the Query grid.

Sort Reordering of data in ascending or descending order.

Spellcheck A tool in Access that automatically checks the spelling of words against a large dictionary.

Subfolder A folder within a folder.

Summary (group summary) The sum, average, minimum or maximum can be displayed for each group in a grouped report. Summaries can only be displayed for numeric fields.

Tab (in a window) A window may have a number of tabs. These are the different sections of the window. To view the options in that section, click on the tab name.

Table A means of storing and displaying data in rows and columns.

Text box A text box is a control that displays the value of a database field or the value of a calculation.

Text qualifier " (speech marks – double or single) that surround text fields in a data file. A text qualifier is required if one or more field contains a comma.

Tool tip When the cursor hovers over an item the program displays a tip, usually with a yellow background. A tool tip shows the name of an object on the screen.

Truncate Data is not displayed in full.

User area The workspace on a computer for the storage of files. Examples are the My Documents folder, a network drive, a floppy disk or the hard disk drive.

Wildcard character *, ?, #. Used to carry out a pattern search.

Wizard A help feature that guides a user through a series of steps in order to create reports or queries in a database.

General assessment guidelines for all units

Before the assessment

You are advised to obtain a copy of the syllabus from the OCR website. Read through all the assessment objectives to ensure that you have the necessary skills before you begin the assessment.

Before you start a live assessment, complete at least two 'mock exams' in assessment conditions, without any help from your tutor or classmates.

The assessment

- Level 2 assessments are usually split into five or six tasks.
- You are allowed a notional duration of 3 hours for each assessment.
- Before you begin, read through the paper to see what you will need to do.
- You may want to allow yourself about 2½ hours to complete the tasks and then 30 minutes to check all your final printouts and your saved files.
- Your tutor may allow you to complete an assessment over several consecutive sessions (lessons).
- Once you start an assessment your tutor cannot give you further teaching, and is not allowed to help you, so make sure that you are ready for the assessment before you start it.
- Your tutor will provide you with a photocopy of the assignment.
- Printing can be done after the assessment, however, you are advised to print your work whenever there is an instruction to print.

TIP!

When you have printed your work, do not move straight on to the next instruction or task! Check your printout against the instructions in the assignment to make absolutely sure that you have carried out each instruction correctly and that the printout matches what you have on the screen.

Your name

You will be asked to enter your name. It is good practice to enter your first and last name.

Filenames/query names/report names

You are advised to enter filenames/query names/report names using the same case as in the assignment. However, you will not be penalised if you use a different case for these names. Do not enter a full stop after a file or folder name.

Headers and footers

Unless there is a specific instruction, you may use any font size, font type and alignment for headers and footers, but do make sure that the information in headers or footers does not overlap any page items. A small font size is usually best.

During the assessment

- During the assessment you are allowed to use:

  - the textbook that you worked through for your learning
  - the Quick Reference Guides from the Heinemann book that you have been using
  - your own notes
  - handouts from your tutor that cover general IT skills
  - any books that cover general IT skills.

- You are not allowed to use any books, notes, handouts, etc. that are referenced to the assessment objectives of the syllabus.

- You cannot ask your tutor or anyone else for help.

- If there is a technical problem, e.g. something wrong with the computer or printer then you should inform your tutor/the invigilator.

- Read through the whole task before you start.

- All the instructions are numbered, and many have sub-steps (a, b, c, etc.). Read through the whole step before you start doing anything.

- Follow each instruction in the correct sequence. Do not leave out an instruction, even if you intend to do it later.

- Tick each instruction when you have completed it.

- Check that you have completed a step fully and correctly before moving on to the next step.

- Don't rush!

- Enter all data in the same case as in the assignment.

- Enter all data as it is presented in the assignment.

- Any data that you have to type in is presented in bold to help you see what you have to key in. You should not use bold emphasis unless you are told to do so in the assessment.

- Remember that if you find an error, you can correct it, but if you leave the checking to your tutor, they cannot give you your work back to correct any errors that they have found.

- If you notice an error, you can make changes to your work and print again.

- Remember, you can print as many draft copies as you wish, but you must remember to destroy any incorrect copies or unwanted drafts.

- You will be asked to enter your centre number. You can enter this in any format, e.g. Centre Number 11111, Centre No 11111, Centre 11111, 11111.

At the end of the assessment

- Check your printout against the assessment paper. Use a different colour pen/pencil to tick each instruction on the copy of the assessment.

- Make sure that you have saved all your files.

- Make sure that you have used the correct filename/query name/report name.

- Make sure that all your files are saved in the correct user area.

- Make sure every printout has your first and last name on it.

- Arrange your prints in the order that they are listed in the assessment.

- Destroy any printouts that you do not wish to be marked (or hand these to your tutor making sure that your tutor knows these are not to be marked!).

- Hand to your tutor:
  - your final printouts in the correct order, you may wish to staple these to keep them secure
  - the copy of the assessment paper
  - the disk where you have saved your files (if you save on disk); if not, tell the tutor where your files are saved on the computer.

Assessment guidelines for Unit 3

1   Your tutor will provide you with the file you need for the assessment.

2   Before an assessment you should create a new folder just for the assessment.

3   You will usually be provided with one file – a datafile in csv format that you will import into your database software during the course of the assessment.

The order of the tasks may vary from paper to paper. In some assignments, you may be required to create a small database at the beginning of the assessment. In others, the first task may be to import the csv file into your database software and to modify the field properties to prepare it for use. You may be required to create and run queries and reports on both the newly created database and the database that you import into your database software (Access).

DURING THE ASSESSMENT, YOU WILL NEED TO COMPLETE ABOUT 5 TASKS

General assessment tips

○   Follow each instruction in the correct sequence. Do not leave an instruction with the intention of doing it later.

○   Do not enter any text in bold unless instructed – the text is presented in bold to help you to identify filenames, text to be entered and instructions.

○   When asked to display an automatic date and automatic page numbers in a report, remember that Access will automatically display these items (except on a label report), so you do not need to enter them again – you just need to check that they are displayed on the report.

○   When entering your name and centre number in a report, make sure that you make the label box wide enough to display all the details.

○   Always check in Print Preview before printing and check your printouts to ensure all the data is displayed in full. Pay particular attention to dates and numbers with decimal places. In text fields, look at the longest entry in the actual database table and compare this to your printout to ensure that this entry is displayed in full.

Create a new database

You will need to create a small database of about 10 records with 7–10 fields.

You will need to:

1   Create a new database.

2   Create a new table in Design view.

3   Create field names and define field types in a table.

4   Format data types.

5   Save and name a table.

6   Enter records.

Assessment tips – create a database

○ Read through the scenario so that you understand the type of data you will be working with.

○ Read through the entire task *before* you start.

○ Look at the data you will be entering into the database before designing your database.

○ Make a note of how many characters there are in the longest entry in each field so that you know the **minimum** setting for the field length.

○ For fields that will contain telephone numbers, set the Data Type to Text to ensure any leading 0s will be displayed.

○ Format numeric fields as **Fixed** and always set the number of decimal places.

○ Check that date fields are in English format (day, followed by month, followed by year). You do not need to create a primary key.

○ When entering data in Datasheet view, widen each column sufficiently to see all the data in full.

Create a tabular report displaying all fields

You will probably be required to create a tabular report showing all the fields in the database you have created.

You will need to:

1 Create a simple tabular report.

2 Insert report headers and footers.

3 Enter a report title.

4 Widen fields.

5 Save the report with a specified filename.

6 Sort data in a specified order.

7 Print the report.

Assessment tips – create a tabular report

○ Read through the task and check to see if the fields are to be presented in the same order as they have been entered in the table. If they are, then use the **AutoReport** facility to create a tabular report. If not, use the Report Wizard (see the section 'Create a variety of reports displaying selected fields' below).

○ Zoom in to the report and check that all the data is displayed in full (compare it to the data in table view). Make a note of any fields that are truncated and adjust them in Design view – remember to check the report in Print Preview again after any adjustments have been made.

○ Check that the date fields are displayed in full and are in English format (day, followed by month, followed by year).

- Check that numbers are displayed with the number of decimal places stated in the assignment (e.g. if one decimal place is specified, the figure 4 should be displayed as 4.0). If necessary, amend the field properties in report Design view.

- Sort the report using the **Sorting and Grouping** option in report Design view. You will probably need to amend the title of the report in Design view. Make sure you enter the title exactly as shown in the assignment.

- Remember that the date and page number(s) will be displayed automatically – you just need to check these in Print Preview. You may delete any automatic fields that are not requested but, unless there is an instruction to remove them, you will not be penalised if you leave them in.

- Make sure the label field is wide enough to display your name and centre number in full.

Create and print labels

You will need to create labels either from the database table that you have created or from a query in the database that you have imported.

You will need to:

1 Create labels.

2 Display specified fields.

3 Sort in labels in a specified order.

4 Print labels.

Assessment tips – create labels

- Use the Label Wizard to create labels.

- Select Avery 2 across as the label type.

- Make sure you have inserted the space(s) between fields on the same line.

- Remember, unlike other reports, labels can be sorted in the fourth step of the Label Wizard.

- You may need to enlarge the header/footer to display your name (**View menu**, **Page Header/Footer**).

- If an error message appears stating that the labels do not fit on the page, reduce the left and right page margins.

View the labels in Print Preview and check that all the data is displayed in full. Make a note of any fields that are truncated and adjust them in Design view – remember to check the report in Print Preview again after any adjustments have been made.

Import a datafile, save it as a new table and modify the field characteristics

You will be provided with a datafile, usually in csv format, that you will be required to import into Access and save as new table.

You will need to:

1 Create a new database.

2 Import a generic file and save it as a new table.

3 Modify the field characteristics.

Assessment tips – import a datafile

○ In step 2 of the Import Text Wizard ensure the **Comma** option is set and select the Text Qualifier to be " (double speech marks). Then click in the check box for **First Row Contains Field Names**.

○ In step 5 no primary key is required.

○ If an error message is displayed after the file has been imported, delete the table and try again.

○ Open the imported table, widen the fields and look at the data in the database to familiarise yourself with the information contained within each field.

○ You will probably need to modify some field characteristics in Design view.

○ Format numeric fields as **Fixed** and always set the number of decimal places. Check that date fields are in English format (day, followed by month, followed by year).

○ When modifying field lengths, make sure the field lengths are wide enough to display all the data in full, otherwise, data will be lost.

Amend a database

You will be required to make some amendments to the database. The requested amendments will vary from assignment to assignment. For example, in some assignments you may be asked to delete records; in others you may be asked to add a record or change the data in a record. Most assignments will require you to find and replace data.

You will need to:

1 Find a record.

2 Delete record(s).

3 Add records(s).

4 Amend records.

5 Find and replace data.

Assessment tips – amend a database

○ Click in the field in which you want to find the data before using the Find facility.

○ Look carefully at the data to be replaced to see if you need to select the **Any Part of Field**, **Whole Field** or **Start of Field** options – in most cases you will need to use the **Any Part of Field** option.

- Check the record(s) to be deleted very carefully as there may be several records containing similar data – remember that you cannot undo a delete action!

- When making amendments, widen the fields to display all the data.

- After making amendments, click in the last blank row to avoid accidental amendments.

Create queries

You will need to create queries on the imported database and in some assignments you may also need to create queries on the database you create.

You will need to:

1 Use comparison operators.

2 Use range criteria.

3 Use logical criteria.

4 Create a calculated field.

5 Use wildcard criteria.

6 Combine criteria to create a query.

7 Save the query with a specified name.

Assessment tips – create queries

- Read the entire step relating to the query before you start.

- Look at the data in the table to see how the data has been entered (for example, if you are asked to find all the records that contain SUN, is SUN the only data if the field, or will you need to use a wildcard?).

- Take care to enter the criteria with one hundred per cent accuracy. However, you do not need to match case when entering criteria in a query.

- When queries contain multiple criteria, run the query at each stage to check that the correct data has been found.

- Remember using the criteria BETWEEN *includes* the number/dates entered.

- When calculating percentages in calculated fields, you must enter the number in decimal format (e.g. 0.05 for 5%).

Create a variety of reports displaying selected fields

You will need to create a variety of reports in both landscape and portrait orientation. Most reports will be based on the queries you have created. At least one report will require you to group data on at least one field, and you will probably be required to display a group summary. Most reports will require the data in at least one field to be sorted.

You will need to:

1 Create tabular reports.

2 Create columnar reports.

3 Create grouped reports.

4 Display group summaries.

5 Set the report orientation.

6 Create text labels and enter text.

7 Select and move controls.

8 Insert report headers and footers.

9 Enter a report title.

10 Widen fields.

11 Save the report with a specified filename.

12 Sort data in a specified order.

13 Print the report.

Assessment tips – create reports

○ Read through the entire step/task before using the wizard to create the report.

○ Make sure you select the correct query/table on which to base the report.

○ Take care when selecting the fields to be displayed – make sure that all the requested fields (and no more) are selected.

○ Do not sort reports in the Report Wizard – perform any sorting using the **Sorting and Grouping** option in report Design view.

○ When sorting grouped reports, take care *not* to remove any grouping options.

○ When summaries are displayed, additional unrequested information may also be displayed – these unwanted labels may be deleted in report Design view. However, unless you are instructed to remove additional data, you will not be penalised if this information is also displayed.

○ Zoom in to the report and check that all the data is displayed in full (compare it to the data in the open query). Make a note of any fields that are truncated and adjust them in Design view – remember to check the report in Print Preview again after any adjustments have been made.

○ Check that the date fields are displayed in full and are in English format (day, followed by month, followed by year).

○ Check that numbers are displayed with the number of decimal places stated in the assignment (e.g. if one decimal place is specified, the figure 4 should be displayed as 4.0). If necessary, amend the field properties in Report Design view.

- You will probably need to amend the title of the report in Design view. Make sure you enter the title exactly as shown in the assignment.

- Remember that the date and page number(s) will be displayed automatically – you just need to check these in Print Preview. You may delete any automatic fields that are not requested but, unless there is an instruction to remove them, you will not be penalised if you leave them in.

- Make sure that any label fields are wide enough to display the information in full.

- Check that the report will be printed on no more than the specified number of pages (printing on fewer than the number of pages specified is fine, but do check that you have all the required records). The page margins may be adjusted to display more records on a page and/or the font size of the report headings/field headings or data may be changed.

- Always make a final check in Print Preview before printing the report.

Good luck!

Index